WHY?

OBSERVE AND PRESERVE, A BIOGRAPHY OF EVIL

BETTYE P. MAHAN

iUniverse LLC
Bloomington

WHY?
OBSERVE AND PRESERVE, A BIOGRAPHY OF EVIL

iUniverse books may be ordered through booksellers or by contacting:

iUniverse LLC
1663 Liberty Drive
Bloomington, IN 47403
www.iuniverse.com
1-800-Authors (1-800-288-4677)

Because of the dynamic nature of the Internet, any web addresses or links contained in this book may have changed since publication and may no longer be valid. The views expressed in this work are solely those of the author and do not necessarily reflect the views of the publisher, and the publisher hereby disclaims any responsibility for them.

Any people depicted in stock imagery provided by Thinkstock are models, and such images are being used for illustrative purposes only. Certain stock imagery © Thinkstock.

ISBN: 978-1-4917-2094-3 (sc)
ISBN: 978-1-4917-2095-0 (e)

Library of Congress Control Number: 2014900592

Printed in the United States of America.

iUniverse rev. date: 01/22/2014

INTRODUCTION

I have had the luck and pleasure to have had a wonderful, full life. It has been educational, fun, unusual and sometimes frightening. All of it has been a blessing of God and my heritage.

This collection is simply a release of memories and thoughts about events in my lifetime, mainly since World War II. The world has monumentally changed during that period of time. Our world today would be unrecognizable to my grandparents if they could stand in an area they knew well or look at an atlas of today's Earth. The evolution of progress to them would be unbelievable. The benefits to life on our planet, and probably beyond, are magnificent, for which I am far too lax in thanking God.

The other side is that time frame has seen the illumination and creation of some of the very worst capabilities of the human species. My reflections may not be accurate in detail, but age has some allowances. The basic facts herein are evident. It is up to others to document undistorted history.

Early in 2008 my ears become more closely tuned to the news. Earlier came the housing balloon (stratosphere prices), which began to resemble one of the 1950s era "Become a Millionaire" TV game shows. The real estate market exploded into an unreal sitcom saga. I could not fathom how any real property—old or new, even very small and old—could have increased in value so much in such a short period of time, maybe in less than a decade. Along with that, the news programs kept repeating a name I knew nothing about nor had an interest in knowing.

As an afterthought, the much more familiar name of Hillary Clinton became almost a daily subject, along with a rehash of most of her history. After the disgusting character sliming of both names, it was a big surprise to learn the little known senator from Illinois was the Democratic National Committee's choice for the Oval Office instead of Ms. Clinton. As things stand now, this may turn out to be the death of what once was an honorable American political party.

With the unreal reality of the 2008 campaign for the top dog spot in the White House, my thoughts have continued to reflect on how any intelligent U.S. leader could not have prevented the catastrophe that has gripped out nation and the world since that time. At least Hillary is an experienced politician.

Like many other Americans, I can only reflect on the good and the bad actions in our government during my lifetime. As time has passed, only stupidity has given way to the monumental mess that has been created, possibly with the help of outsiders who hate our way of life.

What does it mean when the individuals we elect as our representatives and leaders care more about the politics than patriotism? The enormous scale of greed, deception, and plain stupidity in our government that has come to light is mind blogging. Hindsight opens a lot of eyes, as well as the wounds of the blame game. The resulting aftermath is incomprehensible to most honest people. I am just one of the many who share the same observations, conclusions and fear of worse to come.

In God we trust!

chapter 1
SMOKE AND MIRRORS BIG TIME

After the Clinton prime time soap opera of the early 90s, most of the media's political news bites went to automatic delete in my head by 2008. Then the unusual name of Obama started popping up with no memorable substance, along with Hillary Clinton and others, including Governor Mark Sanford of South Carolina, with the usual tabloid type framing. In time, the disappearance of Sanford, reported in the Appalachian mountain area, aroused attention, and media turned it into a full blown scandal. Eventually John Edwards, Hillary Clinton, and Obama were touted as the Democratic National Committee's top choices from the Heinz 57 group of candidates vying for the 2008 Presidential campaign. At the same time, Republican Sanford's episode became a daily report. Along came the more disgusting performance of John Edwards and the evening news looked like episodes of "The Good Wife" or the 60s/70s "Dallas" TV series.

With the resignation of Governor Sanford, his name faded from headlines while the halo illumination of other forerunners from various political parties emerged. In the early days of the primary some of my family favored either Hillary or John Edwards. The handsome John Edwards of North Carolina, with his smiling, supportive wife Elizabeth, became the liberal icon of the saintly American political family.

Barack Obama began to appear as often as daily weather reports in the spring of 2008, but with zero achievement notes. I even asked someone "What are his qualifications to be a U. S. Presidential candidate?" The answer was he had written a book. With what we have learned, and not learned about the facts and background of "Dreams From My Father," the book only offers a Presidential question mark for history.

The media profile of Barack Obama includes eight years as an Illinois state senator (1996-2004), and four years as a U. S. senator, (2005-2008), but no achievement highlights as either, other than a vocal "present" whenever in attendance. The publicly listed scholastic records indicate that Obama attended Occidental College in California under the name Barry Soetoro for two years, transferred to Columbia University in New York under the same name and graduated in 1983 with a political science degree. With few personal facts and interesting scholastic associations, Obama is listed as a member of various groups while attending Harvard Law School in 1988. Then he became president of the Harvard Law Review and graduated magna cum laude in 1991. (The B.H.O. scholastic records have yet to be produced for public scrutiny.) Our current President is considered smart as well as a great teleprompter orator and secret manipulator of both words and actions. After graduation he initially worked as a "community organizer."

Unfortunately, in today's world that title has come to imply intimidation. However, solid Barack Obama facts are as elusive as documenting evidence of a Colonial-era witch. So be it! Maybe time will tell.

After John Edwards dropped out of the race, the political character bashing between Hillary and Barack Obama became a "Monday Night Raw" knock out match in earnest. Sadly, the media kept John and Elizabeth Edwards in their sights because of her cancer diagnosis, or possibly because of what eventually became public knowledge about the real John Edwards. In politics there is more than one side to every candidate. Sanford and Edwards became the tabloid bookends of the 2008 Presidential campaign.

Neither Bill, my husband, nor I have ever been politically oriented, much less astute. Bill was raised by Republican parents. I grew up in a Democrat household. As adults, we have made our voting decisions based on who presented policies we both felt best for any and all issues according to our national laws and philosophies, not according to party lines. During our early days together I paid little attention to anything outside of family and personal interests. The most excitement we experienced was our kids, moving across country, the occasional vacation, choosing a replacement car, looking for a home we could afford, acquiring new TVs and watching TV shows!

I remember only one book from my early days in Texas—a favorite, which I kept for many years of my adulthood. It was the two-inch thick blue "Bible Stories" filled with beautiful color pictures. Sadly, somewhere in one of our several moves, my beloved book disappeared. I also had favorite fairy tales, like "Aladdin and The Magic Lamp," another about a magic carpet, and "Ali Baba and the Forty Thieves." That now seems strange considering some of the terror we have experienced on our homeland and elsewhere, which originated in the Middle East—the setting of those fairy tales.

The only President I knew well in my teenage years was Franklin Delano Roosevelt. I remember overwhelming sadness and tears at his death, along with most of our shocked nation. The most interest and knowledge of anything political that I retained, I think, was imbedded during the national time of mourning following his death. Other than the magnificent Truman, politicians who followed FDR left little imprint, except for Eisenhower. Mainly, because of his WWII military record, Eisenhower proved to be an unimpressive President except for his actions in attempting to desegregate public schools. Then there was Adali Stevenson, who will be remembered for media coverage of the big hole in his sole of his shoe. I don't even remember which party Stevenson was affiliated with or what the main issues were.

The John F. Kennedy Presidential campaign was the first that generated any solid political interest in me for two reasons. He was younger than most Presidential candidates, which I hoped would be an inspiration for my children's generation. I also adored the beautiful, glamorous, fashionable Jackie Kennedy, as did all of the media. Any item about Jackie was inhaled by most of her loving "subjects." The iconic first couple and their beautiful children were deemed royalty. Possibly another tragedy was the worldwide grief following the death of a much-adored Princess Diana. Neither of those events can be comprehended by the good members of the human race. These tragedies, along with others we have experienced, are indications of the hate and envy that has infected our world.

Kennedy's assassination stunned an unbelieving nation. I suppose the world turned, as usual, but seemingly in slow motion. The extensive media coverage of rumors and news did not bring either relief or answers anyone wanted to hear. Some of us cried for weeks, through all the horrible and beautiful ceremonies that followed and seemed to last forever. To me, a transplanted Texan, it seemed unthinkable that anyone as dull and uninteresting as Lyndon B. Johnson and Lady Bird would succeed JFK and his adored Jackie.

The passage of time fills a lot of gaps in knowledge, often with some things we would rather not learn. That is the human race. That also is the political world.

As it has been said, at this point in time, our country has been radically changed into the current downward spiral toward oblivion like so many other societies in the history of planet Earth. The hope and change Barack Obama promised is very obviously completely alien to our nation's heritage, beliefs, laws, and philosophies. Most of our citizens now realize this fact, and probably most people in the rest of the world who believe in individual freedoms. Obama's dictatorship since Inauguration Day 2009 is the direct opposite of what voters were told. What he has accomplished may have been the beginning of a cunning change created by other minds long ago. What we were told was not what we got! That was just a figment of our collective imagination.

So far, all actions or achievements coming out of the Obama Oval Office that have been open to public scrutiny, as well as most that have transpired behind closed doors, have been along the lines of socialism instead of based upon our Founders' Constitutional framework. It is clear there has been, over a long period of time, the intentional distortion of all truth, history, and law in our country. Possibly, that has been a slow, but systematic process, driven by those seeking control and greed. That also may have evolved long before my lifetime. Some of the citizens of our United States of America have discovered since WWII that the freedoms guaranteed by the U. S. Constitution, Bill of Rights and the Declaration of Independence have been diminished and or even eliminated, and redefined with new standards in our society. Those freedoms were established as inalienable rights by the Founders of our country after the Revolutionary War. For example, the freedoms of religion, speech, federal sovereign border protection from foreign intruders, law enforcement efforts against crime, an individual's right to own protective, or more honestly, defensive arms, are now being actively and unlawfully eliminated. Why?

Some of our laws are no longer Constitutional. Many laws have slowly, almost silently, been enacted or changed by people we don't even know in that place a lot of us don't know either, except in pictures. And that's Washington, D.C. Some of the political stuff we hear and read about seems to suggest those strangers in our nation's capitol are inaugurating changes in the basic lawful structure of governing our nation to those aligned to a foreign governing process. Has the education process in the U. S. become so bad that our citizens, especially those we elect to serve and protect us, no longer know why early colonists engaged in the Revolutionary War? What has happened to the Democratic Republic nation established by God and our Founding Fathers?

Those who are elected by the people to represent U. S. legal citizens have, without the voice of the people, much less a vote of the people, illegally changed some of our rightful Constitutional laws to their advantage. It now appears that we are being controlled by anti-American elected officials. When did this country secede to the Soviet Union, Cuba, Saudi Arabia, Iran, Egypt, Syria, Libya, North Korea or China?

By the end of our Civil War, both Union and Confederate survivors suffered terrible death and property losses. Wikipedia and history books report that during the Reconstruction some unscrupulous characters emerged. Those suffering in the southern states called them carpetbaggers—believing they came from the Union. As far as is known, the carpetbaggers played no favorites. The name was a derogatory term, which reflected luggage made from used carpet carried by strangers into the war torn areas with the intent of exploiting people in dire situations. The Republicans of that time were blamed as well for the manipulation and control of former Confederate states for their own financial power and gain. Carpetbaggers were seen as insidious Northern outsiders with questionable objectives meddling in local politics, buying up plantations at rock bottom prices and generally taking advantage of Southerners. However, many Northern and Southern survivors shared a modernizing vision of upgrading the Southern economy and society with one that would replace the inefficient plantation regime with job-creating railroads, factories and more efficient farming methods. They actively promoted public schools and created numerous colleges and universities. But, many residents in the southern states maintained their party values and affiliations for decades, possibly until WWI, WWII or later. For the most part, it was after President Eisenhower began to enforce desegregation that the Southern states' population began to adopt the more conservative values.

According to a Wikipedia article, Socialism as an organized political movement in the United States began with "utopian communities" in the early 19th Century and later became closely tied to the Socialist Labor Party (founded in 1876 in Newark, NJ). The Revolutionary European type of thinking gained momentum and support from oppressed and distressed workers.

The Socialist Party managed to run hundreds of candidates for various political positions around our nation for several decades.

An ideology known today as democratic socialism was created in our country based on the eventual goal of the movement to give control of production to the working class and, in particular, to transfer ownership of major industries to their respective employees, relinquishing "capital to those who create it." Their mantra is to "achieve their goals by winning elections" (rather than organizing a revolution or a general strike, as other socialists in our country wish to do, not unlike, you guessed it, labor unions.) A current event possibly along those lines is the recent strike of teachers, authorized by the teachers union in the Chicago, Illinois school district.

Our nation, as a Democratic Republic, no longer projects the unduplicated, iconic radiance we once were taught by teachers in the learning institutions of our country. Why? When were some of the true facts of history erased from our educational systems and textbooks?

The laws of our land were constructed by the Founders to protect and serve the citizens of this country—all faiths, ethnic backgrounds and nationalities.

Why has it come about that legislators, elected by the vote of legal citizens, are totally ignoring and breaking our U. S. Constitutional laws and have been for decades?

How can it be possible that the eyes and ears of our citizens have been closed to what now seems to be blatant corruption of some of those elected officials whose oaths of office have come to be just rhetoric in all political parties? Why are the principles, responsibilities and freedom of choices, which have sustained our country for more than 230 years, in jeopardy of annihilation? If the United States is to survive, all citizens need to take responsible, peaceful action to eliminate the causes of the erosion in the basic principles of the foundation of our democratic republic. The suffering and hardship, as a result of that erosion, must end or there will be no freedoms left for future generations of our nation, and possibly the world.

From the earlier research I mentioned, it seems that drive for power in this country began as early as the post-Civil War days. Possibly it started with some who could not accept the outcome of the conflict over Abraham Lincoln's "all people are created equal." And it led to unscrupulous individuals taking advantage of the devastation following the Civil War.

The worst element of the governmental control travesty appears to be infiltration, or infection, of every level of our educational system, social structure, and government operations. That evil deception in our frayed social structure was and still has not been realized by many unknowing U. S. citizens.

I find it hard to accept what has happened in our country, especially in our educational system. Some parents (and citizens in general) seem to have come to realize that slow, deliberate, almost subliminal, brainwashing by the unions that teachers are "required" to join has been absorbed into the university and college areas of education. I believe it has had a very detrimental influence on all levels of the educational process because recorded expenditures of those unions have gradually escalated more toward administration procedures and perks than toward proficient merit selection and rating of union member teachers. The U. S. level of public education has consistently declined since the 1950s. That connection to professors and teachers, who teach the teachers, in our public and private English language educational institutions may have started even before the last century. Why?

The creativeness of new and longtime citizens of the U. S. after WWII was the envy of many other cultures on our planet.

In the post-WWII era many U. S. school systems were rated among the highest, according to the ranking graphs of the time. In various 2010 rating charts of U. S. education levels of the students, our country now has one of the lowest rankings in the world. The desire for knowledge appears to have been replaced by more tangible accomplishments with both leaders and followers in the human race. I have heard that distorted versions of educational and social basics have changed the content of curriculums and textbooks, along with all other forms of the printed word, in every beautiful language in our expanded world. This includes what is known today as the media. Why? In researching history, there is documentation of the rise and fall of many types of governments, empires and names of countries—old and new—simply because of the need for power and control. Caesar's empire may be the best example.

It is hard to pinpoint when the seeds of that erosion began to grow in our nation. There are indications of it prior to WWI and perhaps even earlier. Since then the power grab in our government has become bloated with the basics of greed: money, status, land, and, in some governments on our Earth, religious domination. But the primary goal is greed and power.

After our Civil War there were enormous reconstruction needs in the north and south, as well as families divided by lifestyles and politics. As a result, the individuals referred to as carpetbaggers brought in money and schemes to take advantage of the devastation inflicted on the surviving civilians and veterans. Their purpose was to gain control of individual properties and whole communities.

Slavery had ended, even for those who did not want nor know how to be responsible for their own lives. The unseen parasite of greed would bring a different type of slavery to an unsuspecting population trying to begin life anew. The need for power in our young country has escalated with time and the so-called evolution of progress.

Slowly, but not easily, the people of the United States came together as one nation following the Civil War. Some of the wounds of that conflict took a long time to heal. Some never went away and yet the basic principles of our country, with love of freedom and hope, grew with new generations. Within our boundaries, expanding land explorations and increasing population evolved new states, laws, and people capable and motivated to accomplish prosperous new futures.

In the first days of the 20th Century the brilliance of the creative diversity of our nation's population began to emerge and produce some of the most beneficial products of intelligence and freedom the human race has ever achieved. The modern world was beginning life as a garden of new blooms opening for our Earth to freely partake and enjoy.

In those early days, the seeds of dissatisfaction, unrest, and greed were also growing in other cultures. Some of the dissatisfaction, to a large extent, had to have been based on envy and jealously, which only fuels the greed of tyranny, and ignores the oppressed democratic freedom. In our republic, democracy fuels competition and accomplishment. At the same time, those freedoms allow the selfish desires for power and greed to ferment unrestrained.

In the first quarter of the 20th century, this nation's citizens became involved in fighting a war along with other nations across the Atlantic Ocean. Research and memory of history seems to show that the unrest and dissatisfaction in other governments had spawned empirical tyrannical oppression, which led to World War I. A victory for the allies of that time created improvement in well-being, but as we now know, little else.

The healing of the U. S. economy as well as the war wounds, was complicated by a political diversity U. S. citizens had not experienced, or at least, been aware of prior to that time. The unknown created a "wait and see" attitude as our country unexpectedly slid into the Great Depression. That is the era in where I have my first memories.

I was one of the few lucky children of the Depression. Since my mother died a few days between my father's birthday and my fifth birthday, I can only assume father had little or no choice but to take the only option open to both of us. I went to live with my father's paternal aunt and her husband, a beloved general practice M. D. in Waco, Texas. No natural parents could have been more caring, loving, and devoted than my aunt and uncle. I lacked for nothing during a national time of misery for so many others.

My sister was fifteen years older than I, single, and without the usual necessities of home and income to take me on. Our brother, who was three years younger than my sister, was just out of high school. Fortunately, my siblings found temporary refuge with our paternal grandparents. My sister married about a year later and my brother came to live with Aunt Myrtle and Uncle Doc. Thanks to them, he began attending Baylor University. Meanwhile, a very bad situation in Europe had grown worse. My dad went wherever he had to go in our suffering country seeking any work he could find, even moving to New Mexico to work in the silver mines. In a short time my brother left Baylor for a job as a draftsman. He also married his first love, and when our country became involved in WWII, he immediately joined the Air Force. He became a pilot and flew many missions before his plane was shot down over Italy.

When he was reported missing in action, his darling wife, and all of us, became suspended in time until we received the news that he was a prisoner of war. During the first part of his imprisonment in Austria, my brother endured the amputation of his injured leg. During his recovery he constructed a peg-leg from bits of scrap wood that he could find. His release and repatriation came when the war was declared over in Europe. He considered himself one of the lucky ones after the full extent of the Nazi atrocities became known.

My brother's repatriation journey was an unrecorded route through the devastated areas between Austria and Naples, Italy where he was placed aboard the ship Gripsholm for the journey back to the U. S. His handmade peg-leg was left on the ship in New York when he was transported to Walter Reed Hospital in Washington, D. C. At some point during that journey he and another repatriated serviceman obtained a switch in treatment locations. He was allowed to go to the VA hospital in Temple, TX (near Waco).

The euphoria of victory over tyrants at the end of WWII gave us hope for a peaceful way of life and creative endeavors of the most unique and prosperous country ever to exist.

Before the advent of the airplane and other forms of mobility made prolific during WWII, our lives were enhanced by the mechanical genius of labor-saving farm machinery and Henry Ford's development of the mass production of vehicles.

Obtaining any kind of news was received primarily through newspapers, radio and telephone. Travel before WWI was limited to train, bus, auto and legs. Lifestyle was viewed in terms of farm/rural or small town, and city/urban types. In the early days of 1900, believe it or not, entertainment and social life was generated mainly through school, church, and family events or neighborhood and community gatherings. The limited access to large urban area libraries, museums, theatres, or sports events was, for the most part, a way of life for the more privileged, affluent, or well-to-do individuals.

Providing education for children was the primary objective in families. Teachers in schools and churches were treated with respect at all education levels. Children and students of any age were expected by our country's traditional society to show respect in both school and church and, of course, at home. Those basic principles have now become standards of the past. Why?

It is hard to determine when the knowledge and pleasures of diversity became the seeds of defiance and intolerance, or when the basic values and freedoms of the only true democratic republic on Earth became the award purview of U. S. governmental control.

Gradual decay of respect in our society may have begun long before it became evident to me in the 1950s. Some of it, undoubtedly, was an after effect of the two World wars.

Along with wonderful achievements, we as a tolerant and democratic society began to experience student and worker unrest, and even violence, demanding more "rights" for the theme or cause of the day. Parents and communities became familiar with good and bad influences in daily life. Television became the great at-home entertainment center of many families. A bit later the words "pot" or "weed" became common usage for our youth as did "hippy" and "flower child." The rest of us were forced to learn a whole new language that had no beauty at all.

With the growth of commercial airlines and the advancement of jet planes, we began to enjoy the pleasures of expanded travel.

Working government is complicated, or so the elected brains under capitol domes like to tell us. Complication covers a lot of fat frauds.

According to one legal authority, Judge Andrew Napolitano said during a 2012 TV show that the IRS was gearing up to become the health care cop in charge of enforcing the health care law (Obamacare) in case the 2,800 pages of unconstitutional mandated taxes, fees, costs, and 15,000 internal and unrelated attached regulations, are not repealed by Congress.

Legislative spending on multiplying public projects is ongoing. Government spending has become an addiction of most politicians/legislators once they take their oath of office. Why?

From this taxpayer citizen's observation, our government and country has now come full circle, back to individual subservience. That was the way of life in England under King George III, which provoked American colonists to dump that tea in the Boston Harbor.

After the American Revolution, which gave birth to our country, the Founders, other colonists, and immigrants, welcomed the opportunity to establish a new home. For many, this meant learning a new language, English, which was proclaimed the national language by the Founders. Many settlements were created by immigrants who spoke the language of the places they had left, so they helped one another to learn the language of their new country.

The flow of immigrants with the desire to become citizens of this land, as it was constructed, has been constant. Those immigrants did not come with the expectation of forcing the culture and traditions of their former homelands on their newly adopted home.

Unlike today's residents of the United States, most of those early immigrants did not protest, insist or demand on using the flag and language of the country they were no longer any part of. They immigrated eager to use their individual skills and talents to feed, clothe and house themselves and to quickly adapt and become educated to their new way of life. They were given the opportunity by their new environment and government to individually create, not only the necessities for their new lives, but also to achieve for themselves some of the fantasies that had previously only been a dream. How things have changed. Another Why? for wage earning, voting citizens being expected to fund not only their own necessities, and today's government operation, but also every desired luxury of those who do not choose to earn income—non-legal residents, criminals and those incarcerated in jails and prisons.

Since WWII, our elected legislators have permitted the practice of giving welfare benefits to those who give birth to children. The more children a female produces, the more money she collects from our government in the form of our wage earned tax money. Since numerous aid projects have been allowed to become gimme programs, misuse of welfare and other social program benefits have been and still are being condoned and expanded by the legislators we elect to serve this country, and those who elected them. This permissive policy enables federal funding of both legal and illegal drugs, to be obtained by those who consider themselves entitled to total support by the U. S. government, which factually is funded by wage earning, voting taxpayers. Citizens, who work for a paycheck and pay the taxes that support the abusers, have learned their elected representatives are more public spirited toward the law breakers than they are toward the taxpayers who fund the crime and vote those legislators into office. Why?

The U. S. citizen's freedom and privilege of selecting and voting for a candidate to represent them in our Congress has been degraded by policies and practices that are more partisan and government-controlled than serving any needs of the majority of voting citizens. Lately, taxpayers are almost daily being forced to deal with new affirmations, schemes, rules/regulations, bailouts and debt limit increases to cover the out of control spending which triggers another why?

Even before, and into the early years of the 21ˢᵗ Century, political correctness has encouraged governmental lies and prohibition of many of our national traditions with the anti-American excuse that our national traditions are offensive to others. Some of the actions, laws, words, and outright lies by those voters have elected to run our country, are treasonous by U. S. laws and past administrations. The movement to ban God visually from public buildings and printed money and orally from our Pledge of Allegiance, National Anthem and other songs as well as written in any form of print seen by the public, including textbooks, is very offensive to citizens who love and appreciate the freedoms for which this nation was founded. In every other country, under all other governments, outsiders are required to adapt to that nation's social and governmental laws, traditions and regulations, if they want to live there, not the other way around.

Because of permissive policies of politically correct legislators, our country now has radicals attempting to pervert our laws in order to ban our country's basic Christian traditions, including not only the seasonal greetings and displays of Christmas and Easter, but also Rosh Hashanah and other holidays, events and icons. The use of "Happy Holidays" in place of the traditional Christmas greeting has been rejected by most of our non-Christian citizens because the freedom of individual religious choice is the original purpose of the Founding Fathers. Those who oppose our nation's traditions are radicals who want to destroy this country with all it stands for and by those anti-American, party first, brainwashed, politically-correct citizens.

The patriotic displays of red, white and blue flags and emblems, the gestures of hand over hearts and salutes in honor of U. S. national traditions has been rejected by discontents, troublemakers and radicals as well as the current White House occupants, which is an insult to our country and the patriotism felt by the majority of United States citizens, especially those who voluntarily serve in our military.

The anti-American behavior that has slowly infected our permissive society has purposely been indoctrinating all age groups through radicals who have been residing here for decades establishing their un-American causes and goals. The majority of our citizens and friends throughout the world may condemn such actions, but this has been happening for many throughout the world.

This gradual escalation in the essentially weak politically correct attitude has weakened our basic national security just by overlooking or dismissing actions, events, and people that have proven to be very dangerous. One huge mistake for decades is the complete and total lack of border security with restrictive hardware. Strict enforcement of the much-needed national border security system is the right of all legal U. S. citizens and a very big break in our Constitutional laws. Why?

The lack of a thorough investigation of personal identification and credentials of non-citizens arriving on our shores—whether on plane, ship, train, or foot—is the reason terrorists were able to bring about the attacks of 1993 and 9/11/2001. The ban of so-called racial profiling instigated by limelight radicals, and defended by the politically correct loonies, contributed to the Fort Hood massacre in Texas, the Christmas bomber found on the plane to Detroit, and the Times Square car bomb in New York City. These are examples of terrorist actions that could have been prevented had there been some profiling investigations in addition to alien ID requirements, knowing what is now known about those criminals. Which is worse in today's world: racial profiling or allowing free access to any and all of our national boundaries to any and all potential terrorists? Some of the inadequate, insulting, and insecure travel requirements put in place a few years ago, rather than the practical, individual IDs needed to board planes and other forms of transportation have been proven ineffective. The ridiculous pre-boarding requirements are an insult to all ages, shapes and nationalities.

Some of those have been modified or discontinued as they have proven offensive, especially to followers of the Islamic faith, which demands the female face and body be covered in public (even driver's licenses). How does the body search sit with the followers of the Muslim faith? Where do the politically-correct stand on that one?

The main excuse for lack of border security for decades has been the cost. Unfortunately, it has become far more costly with the deaths of U. S. citizens and others, but evidentially costs are more easily tolerated in D. C. spending priorities, which include waste, fraud and duplication, by our elected and appointed officials. They do not want to acknowledge the need because of NAFTA and other cross border trade policies, even when those policies have proved to be more loss than gain to the U. S. economy and our free trade/free enterprise system. The government keeps printing Monopoly money, which Obama has used for bailouts, takeovers, and subsidies to foreign governments like Argentina, and yet not one penny has been used to secure our boundaries.

Our national security is just another example of the political correctness brainwashing stupidity. Not too long ago the limited security on our southern border resulted in death within our southern states because the drug cartels were operating out of control in Mexico. The lack of border security has allowed both homegrown and foreign extremists to kill and attempt to kill U. S. citizens within our sovereign boundaries.

The most the Obama government has done about that ongoing criminal action of not enforcing our U. S. Constitutional law of total border security is to warn U. S. citizens against travel into Mexico, bring a lawsuit against Arizona for creating their own border security law, and using an accusation of racial profiling. We not only have a President who breaks the laws of the individual rights of legal citizens, but also ignores states' rights, both of which illuminate the fact that Obama can spout his phony platitudes in one direction and ignore voting fraud and intimidation as well as campaign promises. Where is our U. S. Congress with all of the above? Our country is being allowed to go down the tubes at the hands of an incompetent President, while Congress is hanging U. S. citizens out to dry.

It is unbelievable to me that the corruption in our three branches of U. S. government is so deep, that the Supreme Court judges recently upheld the White House lawsuit against the state of Arizona for creating their own border security law after the murder of Arizona citizens and a border patrol agent. The Mexican government has even started warning tourists against travel in their country. Do those actions make you feel safer?

One of the worst actions to come to light—an insult to our law and legal taxpaying voting citizens—is the fast and furious action, approved by incompetent U. S. Attorney General Eric Holder, which put hundreds of guns, including automatic weapons, in the hands of the criminals in the Mexican drug cartels after it was reported that another U. S. border patrol agent was murdered with one of those guns. Holder then denied he knew about it to U. S. legislators. This crime against the U. S. started in 2009 and no justice has been done since, only more crime by our elected government officials in 2012. Why?

The criminal-in-chief recently granted amnesty to thousands of long-time illegal residents. Were there background checks done on any of those who received the free pass? Did any of them have identification showing who they were? Legal citizens have to produce identification just to obtain a library card. Have any of those granted amnesty broken any other laws while living freely in our country? Do any of them have criminal records in the U. S. or elsewhere? Have any of them been connected with known radical groups? Will the U. S. taxpayers be reimbursed for the tax dollars used to support and benefit those amnesty residents during their illegal time in our country and ongoing time?

In the decades since WWII, government spending by legislators (at both state and Federal levels), has mushroomed with the "what's in it for me" attitude that the special interest lobbyists promote to bring in contributions and votes. That Obama campaign promise was just one of his lies on Inauguration Day 2009.

The constituent concerns and needs in the first decade of 2000 are still far down on the list of legislative priority duties and have become non-existent as a result of the actions and money spent by Obama. The phony words of his campaign promises have been framed for posterity with the self-proclaimed lies of accomplishment and spending since January 20, 2009.

For the past fifty years, citizens have watched taxes and costs of living continually rise to cover the advantages of progress, government projects (social or gimme programs), and no doubt, graft, fraud and duplicated projects throughout agencies, departments and committees in all three branches of our government. The average citizen, unfortunately, usually pays minimal attention to actions in our nation's capitol. We, for instance, did not pay attention to the fact that somewhere along the way Congress passed a law giving D. C. legislators annual pay raises. To their credit, they suspended that action in 2009. Recently, I heard several bills have been introduced by both parties to nix congressional pay raises for every year our government has a deficit. Both houses of Congress froze their salaries for 2011 and 2012. One of the bills to cut congressional salaries was proposed by former Representative Gabrielle Giffords of Arizona, who is still recovering from extensive wounds at the hands of the Fort Hood terrorist. That November 2009 massacre was committed by a Muslim extremist serving in the U.S. military. Terrorists are trained to adapt in all situations to accomplish their deadly missions.

There was a time when most non-military government employees came under what was called the CSRS (Civil Service Retirement System), which began in 1920. In 1984 they were given a one-time irrevocable choice to switch to SS or stay with CSRS. The change was part of the 1983 amendments to Social Security.

I read an article recently about the original Social Security Trust Fund, which listed mathematical examples of individual plus employer contributions, (SS wage deductions) invested at random percentages during various periods up to now. With interest accumulated, one such individual retirement amount would be as much as a six-or seven-figure annual income. Just one example of government raiding of taxpayer earned income to shell game fund the social projects, administrative costs and perks in our government operating procedures.

In 2012, with the phony annual cost of living so-called <u>increase</u> rate, the retiree's pension funds—raided forever for other uses—are now a joke considering the monumental increase in the cost of fuel, energy, food and other necessities. According to a Snopes publication, those individual wage deduction Social Security checks now being issued read Federal Benefit Payment. Taxpayer earned income is now being labeled a gift from Obamaland.

The Obama administration is now telling retirees they are receiving free, donated money from the U. S. government—their own earned wage pension deductions. That's another Obama lie that we all can hold in our hands—promoted by the lamestream media fish wrap.

The primary Obama administration secret edicts, pushed by House Speaker Nanct Pelosi to pass without reading, was the twenty-eight hundred page (more or less) unconstitutional mandated health care reform plan, now labeled "Obamacare." Our Congress did nothing to repeal that mistake or even inform citizens that what is left of Medicare would be raided to pay for fools' folly—Obamacare! Since that enactment, government employees are exempt from the ruling which all residents in the U. S. must buy once they tell us we can no longer select private insurance plans. Are you feeling you are living in the tyranny of communist/socialist Russia yet?

We taxpayers, who pay for nearly everything in our government operations, should demand that any law, bill, amendment, enactment, appendage, referendum or codicil we are expected to abide by, should also apply to all government employees and appointees, including current legislators, the President, all his czars, appointed judges and others in this and all future administrations.

Some of the legislative social projects, funded by the legal, voting, taxpaying citizens, have become nearly the total support welfare cheats, incarcerated felons and millions of illegal residents. Those people earn no declared income and pay no taxes, yet receive benefits some legal citizens are not allowed to have. During 2012, Obama granted tuition in-state funding to illegal_immigrant students in public colleges and universities. Legal out-of-state students must pay the higher out-of-state tuition rates and yet he preaches "pay your fair share" to taxpayers.

The politically-correct crowd and some legislators contend that it would be offensive to non-American people to deny the law breakers their freebies. How anti-American and stupid can our elected representatives get? That is just one more example of our government officials condoning crime, as well as racial profiling against legal citizens. You may recall the tradition of out-going Presidents awarding pardons to criminals in their last hours in office. One U. S President granted the highest number of pardons in Presidential history to 200-plus incarcerated felons, including his brother and at least one multi-millionaire campaign supporter. (Prosecuted for illegal campaign donations, this individual had fled to a foreign country to escape incarceration. But, what the heck, Presidents can do no wrong—right?

In this Obama administration, the 112th Congress amended the campaign donation law limit to allow more funds and votes for themselves. Did they get the vote of the people on that one? Did we get to vote on allowing persons who came here illegally before the age of sixteen the right of making an application to vote without becoming a citizen, according to our long standing laws, or paying any taxes? Why? Because they are prime examples of the elimination of U. S. citizen rights as well as Executive and Legislative branches of our government breaking this nation's laws.

chapter 2

FREEDOM OF CHOICE: FOUNDING BASICS OR TYRANNY

Currently, most of the U. S. Constitution and contemporary laws, especially the criminal laws, are being ignored under the politically-correct blanket. Criminals have protection from the consequences of breaking U. S. laws, but honest, legal taxpayers in many cases do not, as in Arizona.

An individual can cross any U. S. border—north, south, east, west or through the air above us—without abiding by the weak-kneed, ineffective, unenforced U. S. immigration laws. Authorized law enforcement is restrained from upholding those laws by the stupid, radical, anti-American policies and actions of Obama. Where does our Congress stand on that?

The corruption in all levels and branches of U. S. government has become more and more obvious, if not blatant. Because of politically correct social pressure, major crimes in the 21st century in the United States of America are, for the most part, freely perpetrated and unprosecuted while public safety is ignored. Why? Because of legislative failure to uphold U. S. law enforcement procedures, weak as they are in the war against terror. Anyone—terrorist, student, or seeker of safe asylum—can come into our country without question because being politically correct is more important than national security or enforcement of laws established to protect this country and we the people.

Constitutional law (Amendment II) in our country allows legal citizens to defend home and family with a weapon or firearms when threatened. But this is not so in this stupid politically correct world. If the threat is made by someone who looks foreign, the threatened people have been treated as the criminals for racial profiling as reported in Arizona and Texas by media.

The political process in our young nation just over 235 years has, due to individual as well as political and national corruption, evolved into a place of greater elimination of human rights than could ever have been contemplated when the early colonists tossed that tea into Boston harbor starting the American Revolution. Will there be a second?

The enthusiastic promotion and election of 2008 brought into our country the worst anti-American influence and policies for the destruction of our Democratic Republic since the American Revolution.

Regardless of political party, most individual voters must wonder if a more unqualified, inadequate, ineligible, incompetent, and actual anti-citizen could possibly have been found, much less elected to serve as leader of the free world!

Our population blindly embraced a complete fraud and promoted a political nobody without thorough investigation by the self-centered, self-serving control of some members of our Congress, with the total support of the journalism void media. Journalistic integrity is no longer a part of most of the alphabet media enterprise.

The large part of U. S. voting citizens in all party affiliations, including the educated, brainwashed and illiterate, were bamboozled by the smooth talker full of promises that turned into blatant lies after Inauguration. What we were told was not what we got. That was just a figment of our collective imagination created by socialistic manipulators, if not worse.

Why was there no challenge or thorough vetting into the person aiming to be the President of the leading democratic freedom nation on Earth?

The misrepresentations of the hope and change promises have become an insulting disgrace to this country and brought nothing voters expected or wanted from the new leader of the U. S. A. The horrible reality that Obama has been allowed to inflict on our nation has most of the honest among us wondering if our Democratic Republic will be able to survive.

The criminal, incompetent people installed in January 2009 have taken the greatest country in modern history to the brink of destruction in less than two years. Will our country ever recover? The many laws broken, such as printing of Monopoly money without backing assets (worthless/counterfeit dollars), has created a national debt so monumental it won't be repaid by the grandchildren of our grandchildren. I think nearly all U. S. citizens recognize the why inherent in that problem.

Our nation was brought out of the Great Depression with the events leading to WWII and the need to defend ourselves after the attack on Hawaii in 1941, which President Franklin Delano Roosevelt declared as an Act of War. At the time, national anger and sadness, the pain of having our young people going off to serve in our military, the gradual limitations of simple, everyday commodities like sugar, butter, meat, gasoline, and even clothing was felt by all. But, it was not long before everyone was trying to find other ways to help our country and our troops.

My high school held scrap metal and paper drives. Some students joined the contest to see who could collect the most weight in paper to win a $25 War Bond. Wallpaper sample books helped a friend of mine win, but I was close behind her. I made patriotic war posters and helped collect old scrap metal and rubber items which were used by the factories to convert into products needed by the military.

In those efforts, citizens came together into a much smaller world. Neighbor helped neighbor, new friends were found and allies made at home and far away, and stars were created. Fabric star banners were hung in windows with hope and sadness; blue for serving and gold for gone, never to return.

The shining stars created the "Golden Era" of motion pictures, which was the main homeland source of entertainment and visual news of the war. Some of those shining stars went into military service and became heroes. Others did the same, but did not return. More of those shining stars served in other ways by going to the war areas to entertain the troops. At home, they entertained at training bases, served in the USO, sold war bonds and made some classic movies. We loved them all. Neither their stardom nor the quality of basic values, other than technology in movie production, has been equaled since that time. The golden era of movies has been replaced by ridiculous themes and self promoting low-or-no-talent celebrities. Drive-in movies have been replaced with electronic games and boring reality TV series. Radio, TV, and printed news has been replaced either by partisan opinions or not reported at all.

During the war years, all news was delivered by newsprint, radio or the "Movietone" news reel at the theaters which, along with cartoons and coming attractions, preceded the main feature.

One name became an icon in the journalistic news media, that of Edward R. Murrow. His voice, character, dedication, and truth in reporting were beloved by the masses throughout the world and remains unequaled in the media community. His distinctive voice, hat, and drooping cigarette in the corner of his mouth were known in every allied nation. The 20th Century had the best of times, in what seemed then, the worst of times.

In 1989, Bill and I sold our Bay Area home and cars, stored almost all of our possessions and went to Europe for the second time for a year—touring, pulling a caravan, or as we knew it, a trailer. I had two objectives to accomplish other than seeing beautiful new sights and historical places. One was to find the place where my brother had been imprisoned as a prisoner of war during WWII, and the other was to do family genealogical research wherever possible. It was the first of two separate years of that type of living. Bill was on a working sabbatical from his administrative job as chief psychologist with the Oakland Unified School District. He was studying teaching methods and curriculum in some of the public school systems in Europe during the first of those trips. Winter snowstorms prevented us from reaching the location of the POW camp marked on the map my brother had provided us.

During our second year of travel, we camped one night in the city in Italy over which the U.S. Air Force B-24 my brother had been flying was hit by anti-aircraft fire. One of the crew jumped from the plane with my unconscious brother attached to his parachute. After their capture, the injured crew members received treatment at the hands of the very professional and compassionate doctors in a local hospital. Eventually the doctors were forced to amputate my brother's injured leg below the knee.

After his return to civilian life, my brother was asked to speak many times about his experiences. He never had anything but praise for the medical care he received as a POW. I cannot forget that he told me he was one of the few very lucky POWs. The same could not be said by most POWs captured in that war. He also said the initial Veterans Administration medical care he received upon his return to the states did not compare as favorably. Recently, there have been disturbing reports about VA hospitals and the quality of care given to veterans and their families.

Now, everything in the technical age of electronics—phones, cameras, computers, I-Pods, I-Pads, HD, big screens, "plasma" screens, satellite dishes, and all purpose "Smart" cell phones, talking cars, as well as space flight and almost magical medical equipment—is a way of life. These costly items, today considered by many as necessities, are even available for the beginning grade school age group.

Those of us of WWII vintage—eager to adapt to the miracles of the technical communication age—have been left in the dust with the speed of sound. Upon hearing a back to school TV advertisement, my brain hit a speed bump when I heard a first grader's department store jeans cost $80.

This is in an economy where more than 45 million people are unemployed, some are homeless, and so many are destitute with the U. S. poverty level at more than fifteen percent and higher in some areas. The number of people counted in that poverty level went from 32 million to 47 million since the 2009 Inauguration Day. The increase includes many of those who have given up looking for jobs. The "Why?" must be obvious to everyone even if they know or care little about politics.

The 21ˢᵗ Century has ushered in material values increase at space travel speed and a moral principles decline following the path of the space shuttles. The early aftermath of 9/11/2001 brought U. S. citizens together in overwhelming sadness, anguish, disbelief, anger and pride. Unfortunately, most of that unity was short-lived with the ridiculous blame game taking over. The only plus in that aftermath was countrywide pride in the magnificent, heart wrenching actions of the first responders, firefighters, police, public officials as well as civilians.

The actions of our President were internationally acclaimed, but the subsequent events in Afghanistan and Iraq were the beginning of the divisive attitudes of the public and some legislators and aggravated by the partisan media. That stupid attitude has started a political second Civil War in our United States. Another why to ponder.

Some of our people have never forgiven President G. W. Bush for going to war against the Taliban and Al-Qaida in Afghanistan, then invading Iraq. Those two actions saved our homeland, at least until just recently, from another major attack. People have selective memories in the blame game in the wave of divisive events.

The first President Bush went to the aid of Kuwait after Iraq tyrant Saddam Husain sent his military forces into that tiny country intending to take control. That plot was foiled by U. S. and allied military, but Husain atrocities inside Iraq continued, along with rumors about unknown weapons capabilities. The false information of weapons of mass destruction in Iraq was the reason Iraq was invaded, but the eventual elimination of the mass murderers in the Saddam Husain dictator/tyrant family and the establishment of an Iraq democratic government was the result. Once the support of the allied troops turned the security of Iraq over to the new democratic government, the internal political division started to escalate.

The self-serving politicians, who try to deny the war on terror, cannot deny the more recent thwarted terrorist attempts, especially the Fort Hood massacre. The massive distrust many people have for politicians in this new century may have uncovered radical political policy roots that go back many years—even centuries.

Unfortunately, the euphoria of victory and peace in the 50s was short-lived. Along with the military actions in Viet Nam and Korea came the violence, disrespect, condemnation, and even hatred shown to the troops following service in Viet Nam. That was a shameful period in our history and probably the beginning of the manipulation of our nation's basic principles with subtle intrusions of anti-American attitudes.

The 60s and 70s brought confusion into families and schools, protest marches, the use of marijuana or pot, the peace and freedom groups, flower children and hippies. The 60s brought daily news reports of violence somewhere throughout our once law abiding nation. The Charles Manson murders, then the People's Liberation

Army and the Patty Hearst kidnapping, along with the rise of radical Black Panther and other groups caused widespread disbelief that such horrors could be happening in our country.

Clothing—with the coming age of the Baby Boomer generation— was dominated by faded, frayed, ragged, and sometimes, embarrassing holes in jeans. Imagine, some idiots paid money for new jeans that looked used.

Anyone who wore any type of real fur clothing was greeted with looks of disgust! Fortunately, that resulted in increased awareness of endangerment and cruelty to animals and the creation of fake fur coats and trimmings.

The wartime development of synthetic materials, such as nylon, polyester, and plastic, gave us unlimited choices in products available for everyday living. Shoes, wallets, boots and purses were no longer exclusively made of leather. Carpets and rugs were not limited to wool, silk, and cotton. Canvas sneakers became available in new fabrics, styles, and colors. Who knows, maybe that was the beginning of the athletic shoes, exercise routines, and gym memberships? At least some good came out of a black period in our national and international history.

The "Big Band" era was replaced with unidentifiable words along with ear splitting noise called Rock and Roll followed by Heavy Metal. These music styles gradually ushered in great music along with great music icons—Elvis and the Beatles. Both are still revered.

In 1963 the unthinkable became a reality in our lives with the assassination of a U. S. president, our beloved John F. Kennedy. The "why" is impossible to understand nor has it been completely explained to those of us who adored him.

Another beloved leader, Martin Luther King was then killed, followed by John's brother, Robert Kennedy. Our peace loving country had been turned into a killing field, and most of us did not comprehend the insanity.

At the same time, assets of the technical age created improved and faster forms of communication that instantly brought us events—good and bad—happening anywhere on Earth and outer space with only the push of a button.

The Carter years of the early 80s are remembered for peanuts, high interest rates, long lines at gas station pumps, and the lengthy Iranian hostage situation. The 80s also meant the return of the hostages.

Eventually, we saw high interest rates drop and the gas pump lines disappear. However, radical violence continued and grew with the formation of special interest gangs, which the early groups seemed to become.

The Reagan years were filled with continuing violence and the horrific attempted Presidential assignation at the hands of a deranged mind. Too many public figures had become the focus of violence both at home and elsewhere. Peace for all on our Earth seemed to be just a Christmas theme, which the political correctness loonies now have on their list of offensive terms.

By the '90s the politically correct stupidity had overpowered our daily living to the point that we needed to do more than think twice before we spoke a word or used simple actions and gestures. An arm around the shoulders of a friend or co-worker could be construed as sexual harassment—prompting frivolous lawsuits and/or getting fired. Our freedom first country evolved into restrictive lifestyles because of unspoken, unofficial, unreal, anti-social, politically correct laws. Is that the United States' way of life so many people have immigrated to enjoy freely?

This once welcome to all land of opportunity and creativeness is now a place of internal petty, radical, reform, rules and regulations, which is the purpose of control freaks. With that, we the people no longer have a government protective of individual freedom for the people, dependable security, or inalienable rights to life, liberty and the pursuit of happiness. Why?

The incompetence and graft is so monumental in our government today that we are able to do very little but cringe, and live our daily lives hoping for honest and responsible government representatives.

The reality of the situation is almost too terrible to believe for all taxpayers, and some of the people we have elected either can't or won't say and do what is needed and effective to fulfill their sworn obligations to the nation we have known. Why?

The so-called Bush tax cuts, which have been turned into another tug-of-war in the divisive territory of our Congress, are not tax cuts at all; just partial tax refunds. They are portions of tax money already earned and paid by taxpayers, (into the out of control government spending) and refunded to the taxpayer. The out of control part started long before the Bush tax cuts. Instead of boosting our economic situation by voting to make those refunds permanent to help citizens through this worldwide economic crisis, the share-the-wealth, what-is-yours-is-mine, legislators argue that unemployment benefits need to be extended again. That means government spending is necessary, along with the tax cuts. Taxpayers get a break, but must pay for it by continuing to fund most of the social programs. We just can't seem to win.

Through the years since unemployment aid was created, it has been a life saver for the job hunters. To those others, who work as little as possible even in the best of times, it has become just another in the government bottomless pit, gimmee programs. I believe the unemployment aid program is a very necessary public service program as it was written for limited time assistance. With few private sector jobs available now, other than part time and some minimum wage positions which offer no attached benefits, it has become a necessary government aid for those who really want to earn adequate wages. During better economic situations it has also, unfortunately, become a source of income for abusers.

Extending the tax cuts will boost the economy. Unlimited unemployment and unemployment aid will not. That fact of life is hard for me to express having personal family experience in the situation in which so many are hurting through no fault of their own! They cannot work because very few private sector jobs are available, most of which are in the minimum wage category. There is no question that unemployment financial aid is a helping hand in normal times, giving relief to those looking for employment.

Normal is long gone in our country—at least for the last five years. Until actions by our government are taken to promote more employment in private small businesses as well as in the large companies and corporations—not just government jobs, employment opportunities producing paychecks will be very scarce. The unemployment aid program has been a permanent project for decades. It is not and never has been intended as a substitute for earned wages. Many unemployed in the last four years have received the maximum amount allowed, plus extensions, so with little or no private sector improvement, another extension may be coming out of D. C. instead of policies which would reform the rules, regulations, and taxation which has choked private industry and driven those sources overseas. The Obama administration policies have promoted outsourcing to locations which have lower taxes and fewer or less restrictive rules and regulations. Obama seems to like to help the underprivileged into the slave wage government of socialism or communism. Remember Chavez and our tax money—billions for oil drilling in that tyrant's country, but not allowed here.

We know now that the thousands of government employees in the multi-level departments of every branch of our government have multiplied many times over in the life of our country. Only a few of those employees are elected. Most do the everyday chores necessary to keep our government operating. Some are staff hired to accomplish the needs and wishes of the citizens in the states each of the elected legislators represent. Through all the decades of U. S. legislative procedures, the elected have created many variations in personality and character in the accomplishment of their goals during their term of office. That means their goals may look different to them than they do to us—the taxpayers.

The purpose of Congress is to create laws and actions to serve the needs of the people who conform to the Constitution's rights of the states and citizens. A Federal duty is to maintain necessities to uphold and enforce those laws once they are enacted. One such law which has not been upheld is the Constitutional law, Article 1, Section 9, Clause 7, of supplying a yearly budget for planned federal spending. There has been no annual budget for too many years. Those legislators, (Senator Harry Reid, most notably, during that time) have not upheld that law. Reid, and others, committed a federal offense against the people who elected them. What has the U. S. Congress done about that? Absolutely nothing. And yet, Reid and others rant about the Obamacare disaster as the law! Where is the media coverage? What is Congress' stand? The lack of media coverage indicates most truthfully that they only cover selected events which they approve or agree with. Anti-Americanism? Definitely!

My hope and prayer is that all those elected and or appointed employees in the U. S. government complicit in the disservice to our country by not following and upholding Constitutional laws and procedures of the U. S. Constitutional Congress, no matter what title they pledged an oath of office to hold, are charged and prosecuted by the highest levels of U. S. Constitutional law. The continuing pattern of legislators picking and choosing U. S. laws they will uphold and enforce is a civil rights violation of the right of every legal citizen of the United States under any administration.

In the more recent sessions of Congress, some of the procedures involved in constructing proposed laws and acts have been done and redone, many times without Constitutional conformity or Congressional accomplishment, and worse, behind closed doors without legal Congressional approval, or Constitutional right.

The Presidential Executive Order has been abused in excess of more than 900 times by Obama and changed the Constitutional structure of this United States government. This Presidential privilege may have been abused by other Presidents, but, if so, nowhere near the extent to which Obama has done since that privilege was enacted. That is not correct Presidential action nor is it Constitutional procedure. Congressional procedure, for which oaths are taken, is to veto such abuses of the Executive Order. This nation was promised by Obama in 2008 that under his watch government business would be more transparent than it has ever been. Many voting taxpayers have strongly questioned their representatives as to Why not?

Somewhere it is recorded that all Congressional sessions, actions and verbiage are documented and available for public access and scrutiny. If that is the case, why are the Executive, Congressional, and Judicial law breakers not held accountable as any other citizens would be? The lies and deceptions the fraudulent person elected to the highest office in our government must be held accountable to the fullest measure of justice our U. S. laws allow.

In earlier administrations, in addition to normal legislative procedures, some of the members of our U. S. Congress have been requested to take on various other duties of overseeing, or being regulating chairman of some functions of U. S. government departments, of which the voting citizens have no knowledge or control. An example would be the financial departments known as "Fannie Mae" and "Freddy Mac" within the Department of Commerce.

Various practices during a legislator's term of office may actually be more beneficial to them than to our country or their constituents. The documented, recorded facts of some of these practices or duties could, and have, proved embarrassing to the Congress, which again, prompts the question, Why?

The damage to our nation and legal citizens through the many decades of gradually increasing corruption and government control of individuals with elimination of their inherent rights through manipulation of U. S. laws burst into public knowledge after the nomination and election of Barack Obama as leader of our U. S. in 2008 without Constitutional credentials or experience/qualifications. The vetting of all candidates for the highest office in our nation's government process has been a practice or tradition, if not an actual law, for all candidates for the office of President and Vice-President through the decades. Our Congress has yet to see any such qualifying documents, i.e. documents from B. H. Obama, much less any for the public knowledge or scrutiny. This Presidential incompetent took our country in less than two years to the brink of financial collapse. Unfortunately, the hope and change we got is not what the majority of voting citizens expected, voted for, or wanted. Resulting turmoil created a divided nation. Intentional killing of the basic structure of the United States was evident in the first three months after Inauguration Day and was well on the way by the six month mark. The situation has only worsened since Obama's re-election in 2012.

The Obama administration has broken most of our United States Constitutional laws and decimated our economy by spending more than all previous administrations since our country was founded. First, there was the Tarp trillions in the last days of the Bush administration. This was the first taxpayers heard about our government borrowing trillions. The spending of that magnitude reportedly was to cover mortgage loans granted to unqualified buyers. Those loans were supported by the governmental agencies, Fannie Mae and Freddy Mac and were supposed to be regulated and overseen by the appointed committee including Senator Barney Frank, who was serving on the boards of those agencies. That was one of his other duties. Overseer Frank stated publically just ten days earlier how great Fannie and Freddy were as investments. Obviously, that committee did not include any qualified economists. Some taxpayer citizens who invested in those agencies were wiped out financially.

Those government backed loans died in a national epidemic of foreclosures and short sales, which was the result of the government overseers pushing financiers to make monumental loans to people who were not qualified to pay for them. Will the taxes that funded those government bank loans be refunded to the taxpayers? Will the jobless or homeless residents have their jobs, possessions and peace of mind returned to them? We all need to ask Congress and President Obama that question. I do wonder if the brain dead repetition of today's TV ads about government backed reverse mortgages make any retirees feel more secure. As for me, they do not, but then neither do the words of most elected legislators.

Following the most expensive, traditional Inauguration festivities ever, came the multi-trillion bailout of Wall Street, then trillions for the banks and insurance companies. Next, gazillion amounts of our tax money were used to help (or so the puppet media told us) two out of three major American auto companies. It was rumored by some media that bankruptcy procedures put partial control of one of those companies into the auto workers' union administration. GM (AKA: Government Motors) help on the one hand with the Monopoly/counterfeit dollars the FED printed 24/7 on the other hand. Meanwhile, Mr. Obama was handing out billions of borrowed money from China and elsewhere to fund oil drilling off the coast of Argentina for Mr. Chavez. You know, that guy who many times publically proclaimed the hatred he had for the United States and all she stands for?

Above and beyond all the manipulation is the simple fact that, as far as I know about law, government, civics, civil rights, or whatever, how and why does Mr. Obama have the right to turn over control of any privately owned property to anyone, under duress or not? Since it was taxpayer citizen wage earned and tax paid funds that he used, we, the people, are due by our elected representation an itemized accounting of where every penny of our money went as well as full reimbursement. Mr. Obama was not the legal owner of those auto companies, so our U. S. Congress did not have the authority to permit our tax funds to be used by him or to give private property to any third party.

The eventual large insult to states and voters by our Congressional leaders was enactment of the two-thousand, eight-hundred page health care (joke?) reform bill written by idiot flunkies behind closed doors and introduced to members of the House of Representatives (another joke!) by the Speaker of the House Nancy Pelosi with instructions to "just pass it and read it later." How much more anti-American and anti-Constitutional law can a U. S. elected legislator get than that?

Such action and attitude has been Pelosi's method of operation throughout her elected tenure and shows how low the California education level political correctness has taken some of those who serve us. To me, that is by far the most insulting Why that all taxpayers need to ask their elected leaders.

We—you and me, the voting tax payers—were not given a voice or vote on any of the above decisions. Our grandchildren's grandchildren will be facing the debt incurred by the Obama administration with the approval and promotion of most of our legislators before the mid-term elections of 2010. Obama, after almost five years of spending and borrowing, did whatever he wanted behind closed doors without bothering with the approval of Congress. Some Democrat, Republican, Independent, and other party legislators may now be fed up, but not enough to give up their perks.

Printing dollars without back up assets of equal value is counterfeit money, no matter how they spin it. And it is breaking our laws. Not providing security and protection at our borders is another broken law. Usurping states rights is most certainly counted with the above. All of this and much more has occurred with the approval and promotion of the majority of the U. S. legislators serving in Congress. That is the largest why to pose?

How long has it been since Congress passed a proposed legislation with single purpose, ruling, topic, need or subject? I have not researched that yet, but my guess would be not for many years without one or more unrelated amendment, appendage, or "earmark" attached.

The last days of 2010—the week before Christmas—was holiday vacation time for most government workers. In Congress, that vacation time was delayed for a vote on making the Bush Tax Cuts permanent for (all?) U. S. legal citizens. That question sounds like it could be answered simply with one word—either yes or no. That was not the case. Has any law been about one topic answered with one word, or a law passed with simply a yes or no vote?

What that means is, no matter the subject or topic, a majority of the proposals passed into law since WWII have been passed with multiple unrelated topics, amendments or provisions attached to that law that in no way related to the proposed law. These additions have been termed earmarks in legislative language, which just means projects of someone which will bring votes or perks of some kind to the legislators who get those projects accomplished (passed into law) good or bad for all citizens no matter the cost.

Another definition is simply pork. For the most part the pork (earmarks, amendments, provisions or whatever) provides incentives from the lobbyists paid to serve the special interests. This has become standard procedure of legislators of every party affiliation and it usually adds nothing to benefit the basic proposed law itself, a state or states, or citizen voter constituent. The answer to that Why is very plain.

In relation to all of the above, we have seen, but paid no attention to how our democratic republic government is being manipulated toward socialism or worse.

In the early fall of 2008, the media broadcast the news that the monetary system of our government was on the verge of collapse.

For a decade or more the banking and mortgage businesses have been encouraged and backed by the U. S. government financial programs—Fannie Mae and Freddy Mac—to overextend loans and mortgages to unqualified buyers. As a result, banks, mortgage, and insurance companies as well as the whole of Wall Street is on the brink of worthlessness. Worldwide repercussions emerged in just a few days. How could this have happened to the leading nation of the Free World?

We, as citizens of the United States, have always depended upon our government to be the smartest, most efficient, reliable, ethical, honest icon from which other nations can learn the better Democratic Republic way in every way. However, most of us at one time or another learned that greed has many forms and many faces. Learning the hard way we now know that our trust in the faces we elect to be a part of the leadership of our Democratic Republic government are some of those responsible for the catastrophe our country is now facing.

Greed in governments is nothing new. As citizens, we may have been naïve to believe dishonesty was not possible in our government. The most infectious disease in any government is power. I believe that is what has divided and is killing our country. Obama is only one seed in that criminal worldwide objective, but in the United States, he is now the dominate seed.

All taxpaying voters of any party throughout the U. S. should, before any future Congressional election, ask of every candidate up for election to either house of Congress, as well as the sitting member(s), "Will I be allowed to vote on any and all proposed legislation that will affect me, my community, and my state before that proposed legislation is passed into law by members of both houses of Congress?"

If we survive, there should be some major reforms or housecleaning of existing procedures of Congress to bring it back to the basic working framework as intended in our founding documents, including all ratifications of same. That project and our national security are the only programs—in the situation facing our nation—that deserve major funding. As I have said before, the unsecured trillions being printed by the Federal government and thrown around like Fall leaves is nothing more than Monopoly money and has about the same value.

The economy, debt and our survival depend on the strength of the citizens to reclaim the principles and policies outlined by the Founders, not on the strength of government and self-serving party politics as it is performed today. There are flaws and excesses in all three branches of our U. S. government's operating procedures. Every department is weighted in unnecessary costs, redundancy, inefficiency, ambiguity, and an overload of incompetence. The Founding Fathers must be rolling over in their graves. The citizens did not cause the mess we now face, but we allowed it to happen with our complacency and lack of active citizen oversight. The individuals now controlling U. S. government operations used our inattention, laziness and plain stupidity to achieve control. The continuation of democratic freedoms and possibly much of the rest of the world depend on what we do from now on. The 2012 election should have been the beginning of regaining our country peacefully, efficiently, and smarter, but that did not happen. True patriots and believers in what our nation has always stood for cannot understand how it did not happen. Hopefully, we will learn and understand before it is too late.

The United States has been the leader, usually first and always the most, in giving wherever the need is in aid and freedom throughout our planet regardless of policies and politics. She carries a heavy economic burden at this point in time, but will, we hope, one day return as the freedom-giving leader on this Earth. The giving—now in contemporary billions to those nations who hate us and our free way of life—has to end as our bank is empty. Today our homeland Founding principles are at stake. That is the only priority for all U. S. patriots in the days to come. Possibly I have thoroughly depressed anyone reading these thoughts. I know I'm depressed. I believe most of those who love this land have the "let's do it attitude" take on the peaceful common sense fix-it ideas we know are difficult and necessary in the immediate future. If our free country is to survive with our Founders' Constitutional wisdom and guidance, the citizens of our country must work together to make our Republic safe and free for future generations with the will and help of God.

First, and foremost, there has to be enacted spending reform in the basic function of our U. S. government. The actions needed and taken, no matter what they are, will be very hard, protested, and condemned by selfish individuals and groups who promote reform as long as it does not affect their pocketbooks.

"Why?" reflects the situation in our country after years of being the most unselfish, operationally efficient and updated free nation to survive on this planet for more than 230 years. One answer is that the many decades since WWII and possibly long before that conflict, elements in the basic structure of our government operating practices have been ever changing by the needs of the times, progress, as well as special interests and possibly the infection of anti-freedom attitudes. For example, the Social Security, Welfare, and Medicare programs created to help ease the hardships of the early 20th Century economic problems and established by long gone U. S. leadership have not been properly reformed since then. These social programs are now funded by the taxpayers by way of the later created IRS without necessary timely reforms. The Internal Revenue Service is the ever-growing, never-ending, double-dipping, gargantuan, on-going raid on individual and business wage earnings mandated each year of U.S. citizens.

When these social program trust funds were established, they were affordable and served a necessary purpose. However, the continually growing U.S. citizenship has added taxpayer contributions, but those have been overcome and eaten alive by the constant raiding of those funds in the decades since, for the massive addition of more purposes, projects, or programs. Now, the debt of ever growing new social program put on the backs of the working taxpayers can be hidden no longer. Too many administrations have borrowed too much to support the non-working residents of our country. At the same time, our assets to back up the borrowing have been constantly depleted. In three years alone, our U. S. debt has tripled. The bottom of the bottomless pit has been reached; the hope it will go away with what Obama has forced on our country, does not work for a Democratic Republic, just as it has never worked in other nations, or in other long dead governments.

To regain our Founders' platform of government operation and stability, there has to be reform in the right way in all areas of all branches of our government function, including the elimination of government choices to receive subsidized funding, or the special interests control that runs rampant in our government operations. Just what does that mean? For one, the now many multiple area, duplicated, fraudulent, environmental programs funded by the government department called Environmental Protection Agency. Another is the lobbyists-represented companies or organizations obtaining automatic government contracts in exchange for donations and votes. The days of best bids submitted by competing businesses has been replaced by the party campaign donations. Then there is the blatant preferred support by the many types of self-centered corrupted union organizations. We all know the why and GM is the prime example.

The dues members pay (or else) to some unions go into the union administration pool/pot which just means mandated support of one political party or another. You work if you vote the way we tell you. That pool pays for routine union administration expenses, perks and funding for membership strikes and/or advantages.

When the flack settles, the intelligent individuals will accept what they already know—the fact that there is no government money left in the fat piggy bank. Tax funds we have paid all our working lives are long gone.

As a result, jobs will have to be eliminated permanently. Salaries will need to be cut. Bonuses, automatic pay raises, benefits, perks—will have to be cut or eliminated yesterday, if not sooner. The free money for no work should have stopped long ago, but now it must be second on the list for funding cuts. First place on that cut list must be the total elimination of funding to foreign governments. At the top of that list are those who publically proclaim they hate us and believe the United States, along with Israel, should cease to exist. After last year's attacks, which resulted in the deaths of a U. S. ambassador, other U. S. citizens, agents, and military, funding wasteful social projects is criminal. Those Mideast attacks would have been considered and declared Acts of War against our country by earlier administrations (FDR, Truman, Reagan, Bush, G. W. Bush and probably others). Our country is being destroyed from within as was predicted a long time ago.

Some of the workers on government payrolls will need to be shifted to the new job of weeding out the government paid duplications. Other government paid workers will have to start looking for jobs outside the government payrolls, like most of the rest of the today's unemployed.

All government benefits definitely should be cut (even eliminated), such as the special, limited to government only, medical plans. All elected and hired government employees must use the same choice of medical plans all other taxpayers use. For equality, government salaries should be based on time worked on the job. All government paid employees should contribute, like the rest of us, to the Social Security program as well as contribute salary deductions for their retirement. Lifetime equal pension to working pay amounts is not only outrageous but also insulting to the taxpayer who pays for those excesses. Those who serve and give their lives for their country deserve far more in their daily lives than abusers and illegal residents. Government work pension levels other than the military service must relate only by years worked. Retirement of Congressional members, Presidents and Vice Presidents should not include full pay nor include the same for their spouses

The medical plan choices need to become nationwide with competition to achieve lower costs and help enable anyone to find affordable medical and dental insurance coverage. Government has no place in any citizen's medical history or choice of medical plans or physician services.

Hopefully, medical reform enactment by way of nationwide competition will curb the medical insurance industry costs of the malpractice guillotine threat as an incentive encouraging more students into the medical field.

The IRS is long overdue to be totally eliminated because of the completely incomprehensible format and all its payment record forms. A flat tax is the most economical and understandable as well as fair procedure to fund government running operations. The enormous stockpile of rules and regulations required by all departments throughout our government should be revised and simplified on a major scale to encourage investment in our United States economy, and to help the small business groups survive, keep hiring, and afford to pay reworked benefits and tax rates!

The direct opposite of the land of opportunity is the change Obama has brought to our nation since he was elected. Everything Barack Obama has said and done is the opposite of his 2008 campaign promises. There is now a large number of unemployed taxpaying citizens who are unable to find jobs they are more than qualified to do and who have backgrounds of doing those jobs. Graduates of colleges and universities can not find companies to hire them. For many, the 44th President has destroyed our hope. The change he has brought is killing our nation as well as any hope left for U. S. patriots that he even gives a damn about our nation's free survival.

Companies, like GE, have moved their operations offshore not only to avoid paying the existing highest tax rate worldwide, but also to escape the new and increased taxes Obama, along with Pelosi, Boxer, Reid and the anti-USA control crowd are promoting. Why? That should be obvious to all citizens in their daily lives. The power "elite" want government control of everything and everyone in the private sector of our freedom founded country. A very large number of the private sector employment opportunity companies—both large and small, have disappeared in the last four years, either moved away or gone out of business. Those millions who want the responsibility of providing for themselves find no hope of that in depending on charity or government handouts.

All the Obama administration has provided any of those millions is total dependence on the work of others. For most there is the hope he will change, or go elsewhere, and leave our country alone.

chapter 3

TIDBITS FROM HISTORY

On the Judge Jeanne show, a woman announced she was a member of the true Islam faith. She voiced many of the same conclusions I have reached based on my memories of what life in our nation is and has been.

The elimination of the right of freedom of all religions, and all other individual freedoms, is the greed and purpose the Islam radicals have used for centuries to achieve complete control of the world for all time. My understanding, based on my limited research, is those centuries of human differences on this Earth means to the radicals that Islam is the only religion. Implementation of Sharia law for all humanity is the objective of radical Muslims. Dedication of the radical Islamists spans much more time than decades. It has been empowered in many ways and failed governments throughout their lifetime on this planet. That clarification, to some extent, is why many of the terrorist acts in recent years appear insane to most of us. It very clearly gives more understanding to acts such as suicide bombings. The radical insanity has been instilled in some Muslim households throughout history. The basic interpretation of that warped belief is that human life has no meaning other than to kill "infidels," meaning those humans not of the Islam faith.

One evening, Congresswoman Michael Bachman, appearing on the Huckabee TV show, gave a brilliant geographical picture of recent violence in some of the Middle East countries whose governments kill thousands of their own citizens who "protest" their lack of freedoms, kill U. S. citizens, and other "foreign" residents. Unfortunately, the cause of the violence in Libya and Egypt, presented by a White House spokesman was "a film offensive to the Islam faith." She made the very basic point: that citizens of our country did not seek out the "sovereign soil" of any Middle East, or Islamic country to kill their citizens on the mainland of the United States after 9/11/2001. She also pointed out that people of democratic countries go to war against such acts to try to rid the world of terrorists.

In the time before the 2012 election, I heard of no action of any kind taken to condemn the incompetent legislators and uncaring occupants of the White House. After over two weeks of false denials of any deliberate attack, some of us learned from only one media outlet (Fox News) that those in the White House and our State Department knew it was happening in real time and yet did nothing to retaliate or help citizens in danger. There was no mention by the alphabet anti-American media other than the "official" lies. Was there even an acknowledgement of condolence to the families by Obama's administration made public to the outraged U. S.? This latest traitorous event (Libya) and response should come as no surprise. The White House has hosted traditional Muslim prayer gatherings every year of the Obama occupancy, and probably more often after hearing a tape of the President stating he was of the Muslim faith. I believe many citizens, along with me, see the possibility of a non-American future in our White House.

In the last four-plus years, all history has been reported by the media—all the media. But, the truth of all actual events has not been reported or recorded for public distribution by all the media. That has been the policy of some in media for decades. That fact alone could be considered an act of treason for at least one reason: not making true facts public has affected the United States national security in major detrimental ways. The answer to that very major why needs to be answered and rectified as soon as possible.

In FDR's time far less was proclaimed by our President and the U. S. Congress acts of treason and any attack on our sovereign soil was considered as an act of war. How much obvious treason does an administration have to commit before some action is taken to uphold our laws by those elected to our Congress to represent the citizens of our United States. Will this second questionable Obama term of office be the end of Constitutional Democratic government and justice for our country and those who have given their lives for it? If that is the case, the United States as a democratic republic is doomed. Laws are upheld and enforced by democratic republic leaders, not radical outsiders. The extent of U. S. laws broken by the Obama administration may be far greater than we can ever imagine. A peaceful return to our lawful free country can only be achieved by the U. S. legal voting population and our Congress. Again, where does treason begin and where does it end? A very large Why?

The distortion of our Founding laws throughout the decades this country has been in existence raises many, more unanswered whys. I feel I am verbalizing only the tip of the iceberg. I can only hope others will keep the questions coming. I can also only hope that most of the elected in our nation have the conscience, knowledge, authority and duty by oath to do the utmost of what is right to rid our country of the criminals and terrorists. Someone once predicted that our country would be destroyed from within. Removing that possibility should be the first thing on the agenda of those who believe in God and our Founding Fathers to bring our nation back to the world.

All our patriotic citizens may now realize we will be making harder sacrifices for a long time in the future. The uncaring leadership we have experienced has cost all citizens dearly. It will also take time to make our untapped domestic fuel resources available in an effort to lower the price of food and fuel. Reversing and reforming the current mountain of government rules and regulations to simplify procedures and lower costs to attract private industry back to our shores will take time and expertise.

It will take a lot of time to expel the multi-levels of fraud, waste and duplication in the basic procedures from the day-to-day running of our government. That will result in unemployment and/or relocation for some government workers. Funds will end for many state subsidies, which will mean some state and local services will be cut or end altogether. Most federal grants will end.

All U. S. citizens will be experiencing much of what we probably would not have imagined in our lives in our wonderful nation. We will survive and we will succeed in all that is necessary for future free generations only if the correct and legal peaceful actions are taken now. I hope one of the first actions in regaining our government purpose will be the expansion and restructuring of national security.

Possibly the relocation of government workers will be into border patrol training and expansion. Possibly the members of our National Guard would be involved in that area. Multiple objectives will be aided in that process.

There may be some simple changes which will aid some of the government programs. For instance, the Postal Service, the National Park Services, public auto and rail transportation, and airline services could benefit by employment of the able-bodied currently on welfare. Eliminate welfare to all except the disabled.

I know! I have a lot of nerve! I am just a worried nobody thinking out loud about the desperation that has been coming since the '90s. The bubble in this new millennium was bound to burst, as most all knew it would. We also knew there would be consequences for stupidity or should have known. The greedy U. S. leadership knew for a long time, but didn't care. That now has to change in a big way. It may be almost like the new beginning of 1882.

I have little tangible evidence to back up my memories and very few printed documents for sources. I have heard similar thoughts, words and feelings from others who have, or may have, the same fears and frustrations about the situation in our country.

We need to make sure the United States of America begins the first essential change to repair and undo the damage the criminal-in-chief has inflicted on our country. That is, making certain we the people are in charge of how our government works and know how it works at all times. We can no longer delegate full authority to those we elect. I believe that should be the first new amendment to our Constitution. Each time we vote, we need to know exactly what we are voting for or against.

For as long as I can remember new, retread, or reworded propositions have been presented to voters in every election. Some proposals are written in such a way many voters have little clue as to what either a "Yes" or a "No" vote will mean. Possibly some propositions are written to be intentionally misleading. There are probably millions more Why questions. The questions all have one meaning. The life or death of our country, the USA, and the principles for which it was created by God and our Founding Fathers were totally unknown, or ignored by some of the voters on November 6, 2012. A reflection by voters with any common sense should bring a yes or no, for or against the events and actions which have brought us and our planet to this crucial point in time.

Have the words of promise spoken before his election in 2008 by the person who now resides in the White House been acted upon in truth and reality? Have the people he chose to run the government of this country carried out the Constitutional laws of our country? Have all actions been made public to the Congress of our country and we, the people? Have those people elected to Congress fulfilled their sworn oaths of office and the actual wishes and needs of the voters who elected them?

For example, have all the laws made since the Political Correctness affirmative served the voting taxpayer or just those other non-working or non-voting individuals—legal or illegal—in residence?

Are the federal monies printed going to fund honest, needy individual programs, organizations and countries or governments friendly to U. S. Constitutional policies and principles? How many laws passed by Congress are taxpaying voters actually and factually allowed to vote on?

I think the rights of individuals, especially voting rights, have been violated or eliminated altogether by both state and federal legislators over a long period of time through, at the very least, manipulation of laws. I was astounded in February 2009 when I heard that the census taking procedures were to be handled by the White House, and that the amount of our paid tax funds was to be in the first stimulus package. Few details as to whom or where that money was going, or who was to be in control of the handling of it, was not communicated by the media to the public, until after the fact, if at all. On April 15, 2009 concerned voters by the thousands, traveled by buses from several West Coast states, to gather peacefully at the California State Capitol Building. From about 8 a.m. until 5 p.m., trucks of all sizes and types bearing protest signs, circled those grounds all day. The Tea Party groups gathered with patriotic banners, signs and costumes listening to the speeches by caring, prominent legislators, journalists, talk show and TV personalities expressing the horror of citizens at the unlawful actions being taken in those early days of the first Obama administration, without the voice, consent, or vote of the taxpayers. Why was Congress silent?

By 2010 the Obama administration had tripled the national debt, depleted our border security, and given hundreds of guns to the drug cartels in Mexico through the Attorney General's office. That resulted in border patrol guards being killed as well as injuries to Arizona civilians. No federal action was taken other than Obama passing unknown laws and regulations by Executive Order, giving borrowed or printed Monopoly money to foreign governments and committed numerous other unlawful or unauthorized acts which pushed our country closer to, I believe, his personal goal of socialist subservient status, or possibly worse, extinction. His actions did not match his teleprompter words to the voters and residents, and the situation was obvious to anyone with an ounce of common sense. Why was Congress silent and inactive?

As the November 2012 Presidential election approached, it appeared many Obama 2008 voters were not happy with the results of the situation in our country after four years. The overloaded Republican National Committee Primary list of contenders did nothing to strengthen the opposition to Obama. The many primary debates just added confusion as well as nasty, undeserved criticism. As a result, no major candidate has emerged. The spineless RNC is still on training wheels.

From the beginning Mitt Romney was a very qualified candidate because of his business and government service experience. But, he was just too nice a person. His reality was an untarnished image. He told the absolute truth at all times. His image was not as a hard fighter so he came across as weak. The other candidates seemed to carry too much baggage, whatever that is, and the rest were virtual or actual unknowns. We will never know what could have happened!

I favored the plain, strong, to the point words of Newt Gingrich even though I had come to distrust all legislators. As Speaker of the House, he was a D.C. insider who knew his way around. But he, along with most of the other candidates, played some nasty politics during the primary, which may or may not be standard procedure, but that type of rhetoric seemed totally out of bounds this time around. As some might say, it's definitely not politically correct.

In this last decade, I have developed distrust for all elected officials, politicians and legislators, especially those in California and Washington D. C. Of the 2012 primary candidates, I think Newt was the strongest choice at the time. He would have done whatever needed to be done to strengthen and protect our country. Newt never left any doubt that our Constitutional Democratic Republic nation came first and foremost. Newt is not a fence sitter, or "one to go along to get along." He knows how to negotiate.

During the months and weeks leading up to the 2012 election several basically unknown personalities emerged who could become "elected" stars in the administration of the policies and issues in our country. The most important issue facing voting citizens of our country as we have known it is the individual citizen's rightful legal freedoms as stated in our nation's Constitution and Bill of Rights as well as the Declaration of Independence.

Voters must be the authority the elected persons answer to before any proposition or change becomes law. That has to be the bottom line in the future. Legislators at any level have for decades not followed constituents' directives in their official actions after taking their oaths of office. All individuals elected to any public service officer must abide by, and answer to all the same laws just as all other voting citizens are required to do so by U. S. laws. The best example of unlawful use of public office is the "Medical Care Reform Law," which was enacted at the instruction of Speaker of The House, Nancy Pelosi, who ordered "Pass it and read it later." I believe the legislators who followed Pelosi's instructions did so against the Constitutional rights of the citizen voters.

I believe Madam Pelosi is unfit for office as she was not upholding U. S. Constitutional Law with her instruction to the other members of The House of Representatives. Therefore, she has no respect for our laws in fulfilling the directives of voting citizens.

Citizens of our nation today face major life-threatening catastrophes, now and into future generations. One, the education and historical distortions, which limited research has illuminated, just through the decline of the education levels in our nation and the world. Two, those declines affect the mental capacity and levels of decisions made by all national and government world leaders and citizens of those national governments.

The facts, research and observations I have described reflect the assaults that have overwhelmed our democratic republic principles, and have become more obvious since WWII.

Those assaults on the principles established by our Founders with the resulting issues are the basic factors facing our nation today and in the future. Those assaults may have begun very early in our nation's history, but are historically evident much earlier in other areas on this planet.

In simple language what does that mean? It means that we, as free people, have been brought to the point of making the choice between upholding the principles of freedom upon which the United States was created, or as Barack H. Obama put it, moving forward with the changes he has implanted. His vision is to turn us into a socialist, government-controlled, subservient population country.

Several major events have imparted that trend. Early in September 2012 the media reported a spontaneous attack on our consulate in Benghazi, Libya by protestors angry about an Internet film disrespectful to the Muslim religion. Our TV screens were filled with the horrific fire that destroyed the U. S. consulate and resulted in the deaths of our ambassador and three other U. S. citizens on the anniversary of the 2001 attack in New York City. The news coverage was constant, but with sketchy and conflicting details provided in the following days. The how it happened was completely unbelievable, and the why even more implausible. More questions than answers were forthcoming as monster Hurricane Sandy was growing in the Atlantic.

Meanwhile, the election campaign rhetoric intensified. By Halloween the East Coast started to prepare for Sandy's predicted massive winds and flooding rains in the wake of the deadly devastation to many metropolitan and residential areas. The storm coverage area was unusually large, slower moving than most are and seemed to go on forever. The effects reached inland as far as Chicago and up into Canada. Schools were closed and Halloween festivities postponed in most areas. Travel came to a standstill; the NY subways were shut down, flooded, and some major tunnels closed indefinitely. The initial after storm reports indicated the New Jersey shoreline and Coney Island in New York were the hardest hit. By election day the damage and devastation was overwhelming; then a major snow storm blew in on top of the damage left in the wake of Sandy.

President Obama left D. C. on a campaign trip to Las Vegas before heading to Chicago to vote. Sadly, voting in the storm areas dropped off the resident's priority list. By mid-November most of Coney Island had received minimal, if any, help from FEMA when the campaigner-in-chief finally decided to stop in and take a look.

The media declared Obama re-elected by eight o'clock on election eve. Most ballots remained uncounted and overseas ballots would not be available for counting for several days. It was interesting to hear from lamestream media that in 51 districts in Pennsylvania, opponent Mitt Romney, did not receive a single vote. That, if true, may not have been the fault of former President George Bush. In California the progressive educated, politically correct, legislative disciples of Obama remain in charge. Raising the state sales and income tax rates for we, the dummies, enables additional freebies for all non-workers, illegal residents, incarcerated as well as adds hefty percentages to special projects, such as union membership enforcement by NEA, CTA, ASIU, new ACORN and the UAW leadership. All the above spending is ongoing while watching unemployment grow with the shutdown of the California branches of Heinz, Campbell's and Hostess.

As more potential irregularities turned up after election day—both state and federal—there was no plausible explanation from any in the Obama administration as to why our patriots in the Benghazi attack were not given support or defended. The lack of any action for seven hours by our U. S. Commander-in-Chief is a treasonable act in itself. His lack of action merits nothing less than charges of multiple crimes against our country. It makes the so-called Watergate scandal seem like a parlor game. FDR filed treason charges for far less and would have declared both the 2001 and the 2012 attacks on our country as acts of war. Harry S. Truman was even more of a Patriot and far less self serving as President of our country!

It is sad to learn how far back the instilling of the corruption in our country goes. The recent blatant facts should bring chills to any and all who love our country and all it has given to so many.

Why would any elected legislator who loved and believed in the freedoms offered by our country's founding documents so specifically and adamantly refuse to uphold the Constitutional law of an annual federal budget? Why would an elected President of the U. S. declare mandates the citizens must obey without a vote of the people and knowledge or approval of the U. S. Congress? Why has that Congress reportedly not done their duty, as the representatives of the voters and this country, anything about the more than 900, by executive order, unconstitutional, illegal, treasonable crimes against the United States? Why has most of the media basically ignored it all? These are some of the most recent Why's! The most important why, by far is, why would any U. S. legal, voting, citizen, re-elect such leaders to a second term in any office?

Now, our focus must be on the way we peacefully and legally remedy those mistakes to insure the survival of our nation and those who love her. We should be aware that the self-serving factions now in power will be the instigators and supporters of violence, just as they did the Wall Street protests! The media will undoubtedly place blame elsewhere. At that point, patriots who oppose such tactics will be rounded up, confined, or even eliminated until the radical takeover of our country is completed. If the legislators who oppose the current administration policies don't grow some spine fast they will be joining the rest of us.

At this point, some could see me as one of the doomsday prophets. I just love and appreciate my heritage for which my family has been blessed only by God and the creation of this nation.

This nation has never before faced so much blatant anti-American control in government leadership. The process to regain the basic freedoms in our nation's history has to begin with the patriot legislators of all parties in our Congressional houses now in the minority. It is imperative for them to use our Constitutional laws and resources to begin taking our country back. Those elected by the people need to immediately show the spine of Tea Party groups, both in the pre-revolution time in Boston Harbor and in the 2010 elections. That is now shamefully being deemed by the Senate Majority leader Harry Reid as anti-government. We, the people, want our Constitutional country back and we want it back now.

Although my husband's health took precedence over my writing passion for several months, nothing has changed—just talk, talk, and more talk—with the criminals in control of U. S. government. We have been pushed further down the tube with trillions more borrowed, laws broken, and taxpayers two generations away sold into serfdom with hidden laws passed giving more control, money, and power to Obama and those legislators who support his anti-American policies.

The year 2013 brought more taxes for nearly 80% of U. S. taxpayers. So much for no new taxes for those earning less than

$250,000 a year. Obama's lies are now White House policy. The amount of increased borrowing, taxation and treason are just the largest actions being kept hidden. The bulk of the media ignores even the common sense truth along with the usual support of law breaking while giving a blind eye to citizen rights. I can't help but wonder how long it will take the gimme population to realize the news is not news, only U. S. government controlled propaganda in the chains of serfdom. Media ratings lead one to believe the media doesn't even know it has already gone over the fiscal cliff.

All of the above is not only obvious, but it is also, for the most part, a matter of record. If the economic situation after more than four years does not illuminate the situation to still breathing voters along with citizens of the world, the rest of them must be brain dead.

U. S. citizens, who pay attention and vote, know they have been abandoned by those they have given control of our country. The majority of media sources have not been telling citizens of this country and others on Earth a reason for that, as that has no reason. The newsprint, network, and celebrity bigheads have documented millionaire—or larger—incomes for years. These incomes have been earned by way of the freedoms, policies, and philosophies established by the creators of our country, along with the large companies and small businesses, which pay ninety plus percent of our country's tax revenue. How and why millionaires and billionaires like George Soros, Ted Turner, Michael Moore, and pretty boy George Clooney, would defend, much less, support the likes of Obama, Holder, and all the others in the current administration is to my rational mind, insane! Stupidity, with knowledge available, is insanity!

I have accepted the fact Obama and his criminal czars have reached their goal of killing our wonderful democratic republic freedoms with the help of the brainwashed and the alphabet media. The politically correct socialist/communist policies now just about rule us even if the uninformed, or just don't want to know groups remain blind to their fate! It is only a matter of time until the elected abolish our Founders' documents and laws as the legislative powers have been so corrupted they will soon be as dead as the freedoms they were created to protect.

We have experienced lies and secret hidden actions against our basic laws by Obama, and only ineffective platitudes from elected conservative legislators for more than four years. We have nothing to look forward to over the next four years. The children and grandchildren of the Baby Boomer politically correct generation policies will be paying for those follies all their lives; some born $30,000 to $40,000 or more in debt using the bottom line math of today and those of the WWII generation, mostly unaware, allowed it to happen! Obviously, corruption is alive, well and accepted in D. C. since the November 2012 election. It will take a massive use of some very strong deodorant to get rid of the B.O. smell anytime soon.

The intelligence level of some of the national and international achievements in the last decade are mind boggling, at least to me, and possibly others who are not totally brain dead. Those achievements could be classified as examples of how low the education systems have declined worldwide or how far advanced radical manipulation has become. One of the most impressive of those events is the international masses acceptance of the global warming fraud leading to the Nobel Prize going to Al Gore for his film on that subject. Documented scientific disproving evidence from several international expert scientific sources relegates that award to the status of a "Get out of jail free" card from a Monopoly board game. The routine media reporting for his global warming promotion has permitted former VP Al Gore to achieve possible billionaire bank accounts through his public speaking fees, as well as investments, such as the sale of a radio station to the Middle East-based Algeciras organization. The alphabet media was proud to report Mr. Gore netted a cool $100 million. Gore can now bask in the glory of support of the Middle East friends while still receiving his pocket change, Vice Presidential lifetime income tax free pension funded by ordinary income tax paying voters. No worries about being able to afford his four or five figure Tennessee mansion utility bills, personal jet plane, and other necessities.

Has the public heard of any ERA loonies charging Gore with causing the murder of this planet with his global warming myth as they do the rest of us, particularly if one doesn't favor low vision light bulbs and inefficient death trap hybrid autos in addition to not using U.S. domestic energy sources rather than the liquid gold from his Middle East friends.

The Nobel Peace Prize was presented to Barack H. Obama, and yet, the merit of his award was not made clear. All his handshakes, bows, and gifts of some of those trillions of borrowed money seem to have done nothing but escalate violent attacks both abroad and at home.

Meanwhile, we have to tighten our belts and budgets while the U. S. government uncontrolled spending and borrowing has created the ongoing monumental national debt crises, which the U. S. Congress has allowed, as well as supported without a national budget. That is a possible criminal offense and the breaking of our fundamental laws, just as is the failure to secure U. S. national borders, boundaries, and territories.

The roster of hidden events, actions, possible criminal actions, or worse, is so extensive—both documented and undocumented—in order to see truth and justice return to this world. It is vital patriots of this country learn as much as possible about the true depth of the deception. Those who believe in the foundation of our nation have to become peacefully involved in researching, reversing and eradicating as much of the evil as possible. To do this the "right" way is to balance the alleged actions—or non-actions—with applicable laws or codes.

There is no simple solution. I believe illuminating educational truth is the first step in defining and defeating evil. Many evils have been created for centuries all over the world. My memory of some of them has diminished. Many were based on best evidence theories without surviving documentation and most were related to one form of religion or another. One example is the worship of the Greek gods both before and after the time of Christ. Theory and documentation of that worship is based on the many pieces of the magnificent stone and marble statues (icons of their gods) discovered in more recent times.

Another example would be the Renaissance era, which in varying intensity extended over many decades of years and places resulting in the development of the Catholic religion. In more recent history, the religion of power and greed perpetrated by maniacs like Hitler, Stalin, and Mao come to mind.

The god of the Muslim faith of Islam is named Mohammed in the Islam Koran. Through the centuries there have been many interpretations of the Koran resulting in many conflicting attitudes as to the true Koran meaning, teachings and/or beliefs in that faith. Many of the Islam faith believe the Koran does not support or decree the radical beliefs that dictate that no human being deserves life without accepting Islam as the only religion of this universe.

The many Asian dynasties also proclaim many gods of worship, Buddha being one. Not all have surviving source documentation or religious followers.

Early in 2013 I believe (and am 1,000% certain) a major percentage of U. S. citizens eligible to vote, have limited knowledge, or understanding of the wording of many laws, proposals, or amendments, printed on election ballots much less the many freedoms we take for granted. Some I will name here: border security, protective arms ownership, individual religion/faith, personal voting rights, government mandates. These items and many others are each and every U. S. legal citizen's right to choose, which no person or government can either take away or force upon any individual at any time, as stated in this nation's Founding documents.

In recent years, the evil elimination of individual rights of we, the people, in addition to the executive order (given behind closed doors) as well as outright and blatantly ignoring the U. S. Constitution have been allowed by the elected members of Congress. Ignoring those laws, documents, and individual rights for many decades is in the realm of acts of treason so it is way past time to return to upholding and enforcing all U. S. laws.

Some examples of the subtle manipulation of our education systems include rewriting or eliminating historic facts, self-serving distortion of the purpose for the creation of organized unions, disregard of laws and law enforcement by the judicial system, dismantling of the U. S. military, and massive regulation or de-regulation of privately owned companies and corporations. These are a small sampling of the monumentally increased socialized government and corruption in D. C., as well as in some states, and at all government operation levels, which have been taking place over many years.

For instance, belief in any individual's right of faith brought the colonists to this land, and God was included in the foundation of this U. S. nation. God was included in the founding documents, in the established national Pledge of Allegiance and the National Anthem, on U. S. government money, all oaths of office in all levels of government, and on official government and some privately owned buildings. Evil has proclaimed that God in all of this nation's traditions and heritage is insulting to others. That proclamation is insulting to me and the United States of America.

It has been insulting to many, if not most, legal U. S. voters to be forced to live with the knowledge the elected legislators have used many deceptive, "politically correct," on record excuses to ignore their oaths of office to pass countless measures enabling funding for total support of the bloodsucking welfare cheats, illegal residents, criminals, and just plain terminally lazy non-workers. All of that, and more, is provided by the tax money earned by hard working employed society members. Most of those taxes are paid by small and large privately owned businesses that provide the jobs creating the mandated tax deductions the self serving elected and appointed members in our government system have used as government provided freebies to the undeserving.

How many voting citizens know how their taxes are used in the daily running of our government? Some of it goes to pay the salaries of our elected and appointed officials. But, do those taxes additionally cover the cost of medical benefits, office space, staff salaries and benefits, and D. C. living and transportation expenses? Do they cover all transportation costs to and from the out-of-state homes, as well as state office staff costs and staff benefits? How much coverage of official retirement pensions come out of tax funds? Does that include spousal retirement allowance? How long is the under oath government service coverage? Do all living Presidents, and vice presidents and their wives receive lifetime tax funded retirement coverage? My knowledge of the above and much more is very out of date. A proposal for updated lists of all federal and state tax funded expenses, before every scheduled voting period, should be provided to all legally registered voting taxpayers. That would be a proposition I would gladly support.

It would be difficult for anyone to guesstimate an accurate amount of money that taxpayers have to come up with just to maintain daily government functions. It is a wasted effort since our tax deductions were spent long ago. Our government is now living on borrowed money that it cannot repay over the next two or three generations of taxpayers plus the Monopoly dollars the Feds can print 24/7. We have been told over and over by Barack Obama in the last five years that the reason our country is in so much trouble is because some of us are not paying our fair share. Does he mean the "gimme freebies" group or just you and me, the taxpayers?

The true problem, which has now brought our country to this preventable fiscal cliff reality, is the overspending elected officials of our United States government, not any underpayment of taxes by taxpayers. In the first half of 2013, the media news offered daily bad news for the whole planet Earth. We have had almost constant rehashing of non-performance of previous administrations as well as members of Congress then and now. What confronts all citizens is total lack of beneficial service to the taxpayers. The ever increasing paycheck deductions pay for the 24/7 talk, talk, talk with no action to stop the broken laws and crimes caused by the government in Washington, D. C.

Maximum focus on the indiscretions and/or crimes of celebrities, sports figures, as well as politicians leaves no doubt in many minds as to the dysfunction of the news media and long dead honorable journalism. If there are those under the age of 70 capable of doing simple math, it should be obvious there are some things missing in their education as well as their daily lives. Minimal observation shows they care too little to have even noticed. When the media brainwashed liberal gimmie tax funds cease to flow, socialistic Obama supporters may start to notice that much of their freedom has ceased to exist.

The voting citizens have been supplied with no reasons, causes, or refunding of their earned tax funds which have been used for costs of sending arms to the uncontrolled criminal cartels in Mexico by the U. S. elected criminals and participants in the fast and furious operation. U. S. criminals—elected, appointed, or approved—have not been cited nor charged, much less brought to justice for that crime, nor has it been given serious mention by the alphabet media. Was there nothing newsworthy about Eric Holder's allowed generosity to the Number One daily major Mexican criminal financial operation, the drug cartels!?

There has been no factual explanation for the absence of any protection or support for Americans, including a U. S. Ambassador killed in sovereign U. S. territory in Ben Ghazi, Libya, as well as others in the attack of our Embassy in Egypt on the same day (September 2012) to say nothing of any justice, or even lamestream media outrage, for the families of those involved. That event definitely smells of treason and should have had a thorough investigation immediately afterwards by independent experts not connected to any department of the U. S. government, especially the Justice Department!

In 2008 and 2012 the brain dead voting citizens of our country have twice elected an administration with no admirable background. What is even more incomprehensible is that for decades they have elected Congressional leaders, and keep electing those who once the oath has been mouthed, take actions, non actions, and pass laws that benefit themselves, their wallets, their cohorts, and people other than those who handed them the key to the tax funds vault.

Almost every daily news media applauded the paid protesters of Wall Street in NY parks, and elsewhere—even with the open sex, outright violence, and destruction of the park areas—and yet they ignored all assaults on peaceful, respectful, and clean Tea Party rallies. Senate Majority leader Harry Reid showed his anti-American senile stupidity by describing Tea Party members as radicals and anarchists fighting all government in our country. No, Tea Party members are only against the criminal government which Reid is supporting by not upholding existing laws. He has not allowed an annual budget to be produced or proposed much less brought to a vote by Senate members for more than five years. Reid should have been voted out to pasture and taxpayers' misery long ago for mental incompetence. Hopefully, taxpayers will not be funding his stay at an extended care facility.

Most media coverage treated the massacre at Camp Hood, where Congressional Representative Gaby Giffords was critically injured, and the murders in Arizona and Mexico of U. S. citizens after Eric Holder's allowed gift of hundreds of assault weapons to the unrestrained illegal Mexican drug cartels almost as interesting as Lance Armstrong's lies. No senators or mayors recommended gun ban laws following those events. They emerged only when the Obama followers decided law abiding citizens didn't need the Constitutional right of owing protective arms. The fact that 99% of the gun related crimes are created by illegally obtained and/or unregistered weapons by criminals and minimal "education" members related to the "gimme" freebie population is never addressed. Nothing will change until that does—even in governments where private ownership and possession of firearms are against the law!

Still, it's just talk, talk, talk and no action to reverse unending panic fodder discussions of the massive national debt, the lack of national budget, the proposed additional national spending and tax increases. This should have been a priority—clearly acted upon long before the thumbed nose, over the top expensive, second inauguration. Some of us deserve to get what we voted for, but most of us, sadly, do not!

Has anyone noticed the long, unfamiliar items listed on utility, communication services, or medical insurance coverage statements, or the many "privacy" notices mail you have received recently? At least in the daily stack of ads and stuff addressed to "current resident" one can feel at ease confining it to a trash basket instead of the overworked shredder.

The situation facing all U. S. citizens with the Obama cartel in charge is not only serious, but tragic, for many. Those citizens who do not rank in the "wealthy" group, those who have already lost everything, most of the elderly and recently retired, and those who have not been permanently adopted by the Obama government have no options left. They can't afford to move to another state with lower cost of living. The reality for those, especially those in the already "living dead" states like New York, New Jersey and California, are just waiting to die. The irony is residents on the permanent gimme rolls of California and other states will soon have a rude awakening when the "free" federal handouts stop. If those who inherit anything from the retired who will soon die, the Obama executive order and 600-plus, new laws, will eliminate expected windfalls. In the hidden new laws, Obama has taken control of some assets with his expanded "inheritance" taxes. Those who have already lost everything have no reason to care about much anymore. They have given up on the proposed hope and change. For that they can thank Obama and the sit-on-their-perks legislators.

Is this the "American Dream"? If not, what can be done about it and who is going to do it? Some legislators have become blind and deaf to the majority of citizen complaints, with just more talk of useless committees and propositions which go nowhere. Most of those elected to state legislatures and the federal Congress are now, first and foremost, trying to protect their personal interests. Who is to blame for that? The U. S. voting taxpayers are responsible.

This situation is not the American Dream and we the people—the voters, the taxpayers, and all the others who love this country—can make things right, lawfully and peacefully, with hard work. It is up to us and the time is now! We have to demand an end to the treasonous acts and attitudes running unchecked in Washington, D. C.

chapter 4

DO WE KNOW—OR WANT TO KNOW?

With the additional Whys coming to light every day, this effort to observe and preserve may never be finished.

The other day I overheard an interesting conversation between the grocery store checker and a slightly older young man—probably the son of a Baby Boomer. The discussion was about the historical love story of Englishman Miles Standish and Pocahontas. The man was saying he had been taught the young Indian princess had introduced one of the infamous contagious diseases to the new inhabitants of our homeland. The checker said she did not remember learning that. When my turn in line came, I told the checker that I remembered hearing the same story in my ancient school days, but wondered if that piece of history has been eliminated from some textbooks. I said, "It is a good thing to learn from all history." She told me, "Not all people learn from history." I couldn't resist saying, "That is one of the choices we free human beings enjoy. Possibly, it may have been eliminated because it was not politically correct."

My husband and I once spent the winter months in Florida near long time dear friends, my first visit the "Sunshine" state. Our trailer was parked next to a couple from Canada traveling in one of those classic silver stream trailers. In the course of our stay we learned they, and several people they knew at home, regularly made the trip to Florida for more than the pleasure of the beaches and wonderful sunny atmosphere. These camping neighbors told us the medical care process throughout Canada requires, at times, a wait of weeks or months for scheduled appointments. For urgent procedures, many Canadians became patients of medical doctors in Florida. The wait for scheduled checkup and procedure dates in Canada is so long, in some cases, the prolonged wait could hasten death.

In the days since the infamous mandated Obamacare medical law in the U. S. was forced on citizens of our country by both Obama and the exempted legislators, there has been news of many doctors and others in practice in the medical field in our states leaving private practice for other careers, retirement or employment in established clinics and hospitals. In one such hospital group in California, patients have been experiencing the beginning of appointment scheduling similar to the Canadian medical system—long waits and long lines.

Another atrocity brought by the Obama administration and our self-serving me first legislators is the medical care cuts to our veterans and their families. Those who have served, or are serving in our military, will find their medical care and other benefits either being limited or unavailable. However, cutting salaries and benefits of elected and appointed government employees has not and will not be seen. In fact, just the opposite has been the practice for decades.

Since WWII, little or no improvement has been made to our Constitutional law of protecting and securing our nation's borders. Taxpayer funds are used routinely to fully benefit illegal residents and incarcerated criminals, including illegal immigrants, and numerous welfare unemployed and handicapped cheats. We have learned of tax funded multi-million dollar costs during trips all over this country and elsewhere in our world by many upper level government employees, their staffs, and in many cases, their political contributors, including labor union administrators and other supporters. For instance, some security agents taking fully funded advantage, while on duty, of the over the top, out of line executive level holiday excursions. Another instance—on Air Force One, or Air Force Two—there was a multiweek trip to Europe for non-security members of the double digit staff of the First Lady plus various friends and family as well as security personnel—all taxpayer funded. The list goes far beyond the infinitesimal public disclosure knowledge available.

What is more dangerous as well as treasonous in my firm opinion is the media recorded words of Barack Obama as the DNC Presidential nominee. "I will fundamentally change this country." For the DNC, as well as anyone who knew anything about that man, warning bells should have rung—loudly. His actions during the more than four years in the White House speak 1,000% more loudly than even his anti-freedom associations and Tele-Prompter words. The worst part is the knowing Obama is not capable or smart enough to do it on his own. He has had the assistance of many of U. S. hired, appointed, and elected officials.

For those of us who learn little about Obama through research, he was given little credence as a leader of the greatest nation on earth. For those who, with media persuasion, blamed anything and everything on George W. Bush and/or the other political parties who came before him eagerly accepted and devoutly believed his words. Unfortunately for the Democratic National Committee, they along with the liberal only supported media did not demand the U. S. required qualifications of Barack Husain Obama, Presidential candidate. Most of those in the legislative and judicial branches of our U. S. government have yet to demand the required proof of BHO's qualifications to be President. That documentation is still an issue following the stupidity of the seat of the pants, electoral, possibly fraudulent, self-serving second term vote.

Since that day, almost all laws of the U. S. Constitution have been broken, ignored or eliminated. The elected members of Congress have aided and abetted, if not condoned, Obama's words and actions by not taking appropriate legal actions. Every promise to U. S. citizens that Barack H. Obama made as a candidate for President has been broken, or achieved (depending on how one reads the meaning of his words) and the oath he took with his hand on a Bible, a tradition since the first Presidential oath was taken. Almost every official action Barack Obama has taken since first assuming the Oval Office has been against our Constitution, U. S. laws, standards and traditions. First, there was the transfer of the national census enumeration to the control of the White House. Why? Since then, Christmas and Hanukkah greetings, Nativity scenes, Christmas lights, Menorahs, Easter baskets and eggs as well as other holiday traditions reflecting our religious freedoms have been publically decreed offensive to others by the politically correct anti-American loonies. Bluntly put, the President of the United States has lied to citizens, to the world and, as such is a criminal, a fraud, and a disgrace to God, the Founders of this nation, and freedom loving people on this planet.

The crimes against our country by Barack Obama began long before his phony tale election in 2008. The evolution of his arrogant, anti-democratic freedom destructive policies is nothing new in the history of greed and grab for power. Through eons of time, the manipulation of education, human and magical technical creations have produced a vastly improved foundation for evil as well as good in our modern world.

In the last half century, the endeavors of the caring and fortunate in the United States have striven to help improve life for those less fortunate at home and worldwide. No other nation has given more. We are still giving now, even in what may be our worst time of need. Unfortunately, much of the giving in the last four plus years has gone to governments who seek to destroy us and all this nation was created to achieve. Barack Obama, the most harmful and shameful example of a U. S. President in our country's history, has dared to apologize, demean, defame, and completely undermine the foundation of our country. He speaks in admiration and support of policies and philosophies that renounce our nation's basic structure of individual freedoms and accomplishments. The majority of elected members of our Congress have done nothing to bring his treason to a halt. Today, this nation has had its pockets picked, big time, and is now facing the possibility of not only lack of full national security protection but also total monetary economic collapse. In all the stress our planet is being subjected to, it is not hard for even the most uneducated minds to know that when they have no money they cannot buy anything.

The pockets of the U. S. government are empty. People in our government have overspent, wasted, and given away taxes paid them by the working taxpayer citizens. That, for too many years, has resulted in borrowing money from other governments to pay for the overspent, wasted, and given away revenue. Obama has accelerated that folly far past ordinary imagination. That stupidity has forced the U. S. government to the point of no return. Borrowing foreign money now does not even pay the interest on the money borrowed to pay for ongoing overspending, waste and fraud, but has brought the dollar value economy and our nation near the reality of extinction! Millions of us in this country are not working because jobs are unavailable. Jobs are not available because companies or corporations have gone out of business or moved outside the U. S. to avoid lower government taxes and regulations, as well as to hire workers at lower wages. The self-serving elected officials in D. C. have voted pay increases for far too long. All we hear is useless talk, talk, talk. All the citizens get is a proposed bill for this, or a committee to study that, but no actions from those responsible in our government to control the waste in our economy for too many decades since WWII—the worst of it—during the last four years.

Most U. S. citizens who can think for themselves are fed up with the obvious. Barack Obama has brought about the exact fundamental change he promised and planned. He considers himself the elected ruler of our country. His philosophy seems to have become contagious in the attitude of too many we have elected to Congress. "Pass this bill and read it later" is a prime example of the self-serving attitude instead of serving our country and citizens. No proposed Federal budget has been allowed to be brought to the floor of the Senate for vote by the Senate majority leader for five years plus. That is against sanity, if not our national law, and a major example of self serving before duty to country. That seems to me that some elected legislators are traitors to all this country has offered since our doors to individual freedom opened. This elimination of a free society with high moral philosophies and policies—changed into the politically correct direct opposite—has been evident and allowed by the benevolent stupidity of the citizens of this country for far too long.

Taxpayers are forced to pay for any and all spending. Barack Obama spent more in his first two years as President than all other U. S. Presidents combined. He continues to spend and borrow money without any restraint or authorization, trashing the fundamentals of Constitutional law. He has secretly put into action hundreds of laws attached to bills or laws with completely different meanings. With his secret Executive Order manipulations Obama is taking more and more control of our daily lives, freedoms and our earned money from bank accounts and investments through new and increased fees, dues, or taxes on every freedom in our daily lives outlined in our Founder's policies. No informed patriot today believes the billions in tax money and military equipment to foreign governments benefit the poor and needy in the U. S. or abroad. We, along with our representatives in Washington, D. C. and elsewhere, have handed Obama the only keys to the vault!

Did billions of tax revenue sent to dictator Chavez of Venezuela to drill for oil off that shore help to lower our high cost dependence on foreign energy supplies, while recovery of U. S. oil, gas and coal under foot and off shore of this nation is not allowed for our own country's use?

What is the purpose of jets and other military equipment sent to the Muslim Brotherhood leaders of Egypt, who condemn all the U. S. stands for? They are not at war so have no need of military assistance. Will they be used against the Egyptian citizens who want a more democratic government, or against Israel? Another example of Obama treason allowed by those we elected.

Has the Congress and other citizens of the U. S. been provided with the reasoning of Attorney General Eric Holder in the "fast and furious" fiasco—giving hundreds of guns including automatic weapons—to the drug cartels of Mexico? And now, what is the purpose of the unconstitutional and illegal gun control proposal to abolish citizen right for private, personal, family and property protection? That is the act and proposal of a dictator.

Has the State Department or former Secretary of State Hillary Clinton provided any sane, or even plausible, reason for any U. S. foreign embassies or consulates not being given adequate protective security, much less given any excuse for the lack of protection and support in the terrorist attack and deaths of our ambassador and others in 2012 in Ben Ghazi, Libya? These are just a couple of the criminal atrocities of Barack Obama's fundamental transformation of our country. Do you see the pattern of his destruction? Have you seen any positive protest or action to reclaim our country by the failing, politically correct, anti-American media or some of those high government officials pledged to serve and protect the United States and citizens thereof?

Every action Barack Obama has taken appears to eventually eliminate all our freedoms and sources of protection. On his course of action, our nation is now re-established as totally subservient to his rule of anti-individual, Constitutional, democratic policies, and could include the Muslim Shania law, which has already been established in parts of our country.

For more than four years we have been seeing and hearing the same lies most of which have been recorded and documented for posterity. Anyone can check the facts by any means along with the facts and the figures of the Barack Obama uncontrolled spending and borrowing. Why all of the other John Q. Citizens are not questioning and checking everything being allowed is unbelievable. Perhaps Barack H. Obama has put the National Register and Freedom of Public Information Act under his control as well.

Since his first inauguration, the majority of major radio, TV and newsprint media have ignored the daily facts of the U. S. government operations or have converted them to reflect their opinions. The few media sources to interview or quote those in politics—journalists or legislators—who dare to be patriots of our Founding basics with facts—have only recently publically stressed those actions for what they are: treason against the basic laws of our country—both legal and moral. The few outspoken conservative and republican minds are wimps and wet noodles when it comes to correcting and preventing criminal actions. If more of them don't grow some stiffer spines, our nation will probably have to endure a second civil war—dissolve into the total accomplishment of Obama's hope and change, socialist/communist transformation, or worse.

How anyone with any intelligence or common sense could not recognize blatant lies and not become aware of the Obama treason is beyond me. Is it possible some voting citizens of our country want this nation destroyed? Could it be possible that our system allowed illegal or unqualified votes to tip the electoral balance? Is it possible that our political parties have become so corrupted that there is no honesty and love of country in those we elect?

With that in mind, the selection by the Democratic National Committee of an incompetent, unqualified, smooth-talker as well as known anti-U. S. policy individual to become their candidate for the highest office in our country appears insane. Is it possible the Democratic National Committee is totally supported by the membership of democrats/liberals? That appears to rule out common sense as a part of DNC party policy when it comes down to saving our country from extinction!

IF you believe in the principles upon which our country was founded, then you can in no way believe the Democratic National Committee made the correct choice in their selection of Obama as their candidate for President. The Democratic National Committee ignored the traditional and lawful steps in their selection. The Obama adult life character choice of close associates, moral beliefs and political policies had been public knowledge from his early days in the public arena. The future of the Democratic National Committee as one of the two major U. S. political parties (if it survives at all) as well as other wannabes will come under much stricter political and ethical scrutiny if this nation is to survive the true Obama objective of anti-American democratic conquest. That scrutiny will be absolutely essential if future generations are to know the founding freedoms we have known since 1782. That is the way it is in the United States today. That is why there is and has been a war on terror far longer than most people realize.

Looking back to the early days of 2009, with some documented law breakers in the White House and possibly in Congress, along with unsecured borders, a minimized military, and aid going to oppressors of individual freedoms rather than to the needy and oppressed, the U.S. will soon be classed as a second or third rate nation or it may even cease to exist as a free nation.

My personal daily routine remains basically unchanged since Obama came into my life as the leader of the greatest nation on earth. Fuel prices have steadily gone up, dropped some, then back up again. We bitched about it and kept asking why we had to pay so much, but kept on driving. New cars, especially the hybrids, run the sales waves in spite of public resistance. They remind me a lot of the infamous Ford Pinto. In its time, the Pinto became the icon of a small economic automotive vehicle with multiple problems. The popular foreign rear engine import VW, with a similar reputation, did not get as much negative media coverage because of the popularity of that small vehicle in the U.S.

We started to really feel the pinch after the passage of the Obamacare medical law without the approval or vote of the taxpayers. All products for sale in our country have either gone up in price monumentally, or decreased in packaging size. Many small businesses have also started disappearing from shopping centers all over our country. The unemployed and homeless population of our nation has skyrocketed as the larger companies either closed up shop or moved out of the U. S. It is hard to find "Made in the USA" products anymore. I have yet to hear many comments—much less discussion— by the lamestream media about those facts. The corruption of factual news is an interesting, as well as stupid, facet we have allowed to go unchallenged in spite of the huge economic downturn for everyone which should be publically discussed to the fullest. Edward R. Murrow must be up there flapping his wings in journalistic frustration. In the first months of the second dose of the Obama destruction disease, we observed the acceleration of the blatant lies being spouted by the speech controlled puppet press secretary. It would be funny to watch late night shows with failing media wannabe celebs, like liberal echo Alan Combs, justifying fanatic spending and no cutting of the idiotic waste in multiple duplicated programs in virtually all departments of our government. How can anything be as brainless as tax funds going for "Cultural Arts For the Homeless" in any economic situation? Truth is not what we are being told about anything in our country. It is appalling to learn even one fraction of how stupidly the money we have earned is spent by the spendthrift robots in Washington, D.C., as well as in some state capitols.

Finally, some of us may be beginning to see a bit of positive conservative reactions by our spineless members of both/all parties in the U. S. Congress. It is encouraging to see some Democratic legislators agree with conservative plans and actions taken to stop the megalomania of the self-serving likes of Senate Majority leader Harry Reid and other anti-American morons.

What is not understandable is why any elected United States leaders could even consider being party to the radical, foreign, undemocratic, freedom killing, actions and objectives that we taxpayer citizens have been subjected to these last four plus years. Even the most unknowing citizens, taxpayers, residents, visitors, observers and wishful wannabes couldn't have missed the efforts by this two-faced elected administration to establish ruling leaders and serfdom. That could become more oppressive than the King George philosophy the pilgrims came to this land to escape. However, some of our Earth's residents may not have learned those simple facts in this country's history as education and other freedoms have slowly been changing over many eons. Those changes, now coming to light, are the elimination of factual history from required textbooks in some school systems as well some religions.

There are probably people who have not felt any major change in their daily lives, except in a lack of spending money or shortages of the things they want to buy. Hardly anyone, except the totally blind, cannot help but notice the empty spaces in shopping centers and the boarded up buildings everywhere in our nation, especially in Detroit. Those who have lost jobs, homes and their savings are the ones who have noticed. Maybe they don't completely understand why it happened. Possibly, they ask themselves why there was no coverage of businesses closing or moving away in the newspaper or on television news broadcasts until after it happened. Some did not get even a hint of any change until they received one of those pink slip unemployment notices. "How did that happen" some must have wondered.

There were those who just went to the unemployment office to sign up so they could be notified of job opportunities. I would imagine it was a big surprise when those opportunities did not show up. That was the way it has been in our country for decades.

In my lifetime this is the one place in the world which had something, or everything, to offer to anyone, anywhere, who wanted freedom. It now is possible that if the right changes are not made in the way our government is run, we all, no matter what age, will no longer be able to experience the moral or political basics intended by the founding of the United States of America. Future generations may not know economic and democratic freedoms unless those changes are made soon.

There are some who seem oblivious to events outside their personal lives who will probably ask "What are the changes needed?" First and foremost, the basic laws prescribed in the founding documents of this nation must be applied, enforced and respected by the elected, appointed, and hired personnel as well as citizens of the U. S. A. and visitors to our great country.

Since WWII, administrations have done little to secure our sovereign boundaries both at home and in the world. This present administration has done nothing to improve national security. That is the first law that should be placed on the list of objectives for legislative and judicial officials in our government to accomplish. Of the multi-million illegal residents in our country, all should be considered criminals just for sneaking into our country. By odds, among that group of illegal residents may be a very large number who are terrorists with the single goal of destroying all freedom loving citizens in this nation. The brainwashed politically correct group has gone way too far with its attitude. Not protecting our borders by not requiring legal paperwork, as most other nations require, is just plain stupidity.

In a recent TV interview of random urban pedestrians, each was asked the question "Do you agree with our U. S. government policy to ship the sequestration to Norway?" The answers were varied. "I'm not sure." "No, we give too much to those other countries, "I don't pay much attention to what is going on in the government." "What is that? Does it have something to do with oil and gas? (giggle, giggle)." "I don't know what that is." Those answers were eye opening examples of how badly our education system has been damaged with "politically correct" governmental interference, additives, changes, and deletions—reflected in the scholastic/academic ratings over the past five or six decades.

More recently, I listened to a radio interview of a Detroit citizen, who spoke proudly of his position as leader of the Detroit Board of Education. He said with pride that he was illiterate and felt that was a great achievement, which set an example others could look up to. Detroit, when I lived there, had the fourth largest population in this country. Today it has an employment rate of more than 11% with a very diminished population, including 1 million unemployed.

We, the people, are learning that in recent years, some of the students of those damaged education systems comprise a large number of voters that elected the government officials entrusted with our government procedures to create various U. S. laws. With that thought in mind, can we feel proud and secure?

The Liar-in-Chief thumbs his nose at our founding documents, laws, philosophies, policies and basic morals with his "behind closed doors" and "Executive Order" edicts! A very large part of his words and actions both in public and secretly by U. S. law, standards, and historic policy is as close to out and out treason as an elected leader can get. One member of our Obama Congress even publically attacks the Constitutional second amendment right of the people by introducing legislation that disallows the private citizen's right to protective arms. She then publically expects "respect" for her words and actions which would disarm all private citizens of their Constitutional founded country. That is the first step of tyrannical leadership.

That same lying leadership in our State Department did nothing about the lack of before and after security and support in the Ben

Ghazi murders, as far as the public knows, and has done nothing since that time. American citizens on their home soil have been murdered as a result of the Justice Department "Fast and Furious" lies by Attorney General Eric Holder, with no action taken to bring those criminals to justice.

How can anyone with any common sense, or even half a brain, much less patriotism, not know that our country is being destroyed by the Obama administration policies? The liar-in-chief wants none of our Constitutional laws left to protect the people of the U. S. A. What actions are being taken by appropriate Constitutional laws to clear the worst crises ever to face this nation? Few, if any individuals elected to Congress have ever faced this danger.

I have asked myself these questions many times as well as posed them to legislators, journalists, talk show hosts, in letters to the editor and to all who seem as concerned as I am. After more than four years, it is time to demand and help the elected fulfill their oaths of office to citizens who only want to peacefully take our country back. With all the audio, video, printed media and recordings of the Obama legacy of lies, there is no lack of documentation. Along with that is the verbal stupidity of some of the lap dog bi-party egos who sound like Bidden, Pelosi, Reid, Bloomberg, Schumer, Boxer, Feinstein, Franks and others, who have publically proved their mental capacity and attitude of self-serving philosophy, while building their multi-million dollar bank accounts with the donations of self-serving lobbyists for labor union topknots and others through their phony mouthing of oaths of office.

The corruption of those in control of our nation as well as our lives has tarnished the once honest political party endeavors of our democratic system for all time. Self-serving aims and accomplishments are the strength supporting the tyrannical Obama destruction of our Founder's dream and the future of freedom in the world. We are on the road back to rulers and serfdom. Those we elect no longer go to D. C. and state capitols to do the best for the citizens of the U. S. They go there to spend the tax money we, the people, earn so we, the people, now work for them.

For those of you who still think you voted in Barack H. Obama as the "second coming," you may want to list of all the good "changes" the Obama administration has accomplished alongside the changes which have not helped you. Have you seen a strong, lasting drop in price when you fill up at the gasoline pump? Have your heating/ air conditioning or water bills gone down? Are the food prices in grocery stores less or more expensive? Are you able to find more or less products you like to buy? Are there more stores opening or closing in your area? Is there news of new companies with jobs being offered near where you are living?

For some of you who like to keep up on all the news, did you hear about the 20,000 pages of new regulations which were added to the Obamacare medical law that everyone without medical care insurance is required to buy? Do you even know what is in the original two-thousand, eight hundred-page law? Have you or anyone you know read that law? Do you know if your legislative representative has read that law? Have you asked your doctor what he knows about that new medical law? Is it going to pay for all the medical care you need or might need?

Did you know there are needy people in our country and elsewhere who are able to receive free cell phones? Some of them, it is reported, have obtained more than one of those "free" phones. Just another good cause our tax money pays for, it seems. Even some dead people received free phones, but most of us still have to pay for phone service while still alive.

Did you know one of our long time national laws requires the President to submit a budget in February for operation of the government for the next year? Both houses of Congress must also produce an annual budget. When has this President produced and followed a budget regularly? When was the last time the U. S. Senate produced a budget on time? Does the U. S. have a stable national debt? When will the national debt be paid in full? In addition to the tax money we pay our government, what additional revenue does the U. S. government have? In addition to the daily operation of our government, what else are the taxes we pay used for? I do not know the answers to most of these questions. Can you answer any of them?

Have you asked any of these questions of your legislative representative? If not, why not? If so, did you get a clear, understandable answer?

I have asked these questions of my representatives several times through the years. The only answers I have received are form letters thanking me for my interest. I have attended representative town halls and asked questions. I have asked journalists many different questions about various government operations and actions that have concerned me. I get no answers there either.

If we, the citizens who furnish the tax money sent to the elected/appointed officials in our state and federal capitols, cannot get answers to our concerns, there is no reason to waste our tax money on their salaries. Any of us who manage to spend only what we can afford to spend could control the over spending the elected incompetents do not control! We have not seen any actions for the good of the U. S. voters or our nation. We have seen only waste, over-spending and anti-military, anti-security, anti-American "socialistic" actions and policies from Obama supporters. They can all go find jobs elsewhere. We want our country back!

One of the two major, long standing, U. S. political parties pushed an anti-American individual into our White House on January 20, 2009. That person has sent war time military weapons to the ruling leaders of Argentina, Egypt and other anti-American "rulers." That person has also decreed that a U. S. military weapon can by law be now used by him against the citizens and residents of the U. S. A. on our homeland and elsewhere. How can anyone anywhere have any doubt that our country is ruled by an anti-American traitor/tyrant? Why has our Congress allowed this to happen? These are questions for not only our elected leaders, but also for other taxpaying voting citizens of the U. S. A., only because the actions that have taken place, and the situation in our country today are completely opposed to the laws of our country's founding documents.

The "unknowing" in our overly tolerant, compassionate society proclaim our nation's founding documents, old laws, scholars, scientists and successful business individuals as well as all who love this country "are out of date." That statement alone re-emphasizes the one question their stupidity cannot answer. Why have people wanted to come here and have all that has been offered here more than any other place on Earth for more than 235 years? The radical leftists have successfully imbedded the tyrannical philosophy into education, media, and unsuspecting minds far longer than the "unknowing" making those statements can comprehend. By the time they grow a brain, they won't have any choice but the serfdom life of total tyranny.

If the true facts of history have not been erased entirely, the "impaired" have factual resources available to check for truth or fiction. Emperor Obama is the product of mixed religions as well as philosophies that can influence policies. One way or another, he is systematically seeing to it that the freedoms of "we, the people" cease to exist. All freedoms may be gone for all time unless the self-serving legislators we have elected are not retired permanently, without the lifetime full pay they voted for themselves in the past.

The documented facts of the four-term Democratic president, FDR, indicate he declared some of the acts of treason of some individuals in that time for far less serious actions than the recent "fast and furious," or "Ben Ghazi" tragedies, or even just the words spoken by Barack Obama, in which he apologized for all earlier U. S. policies and actions. That alone reveals the desire and intention of Obama to kill our nation's freedoms and policies forever and replace them with the full extent of his upbringing and indoctrination, or possibly worse. This should be obvious to any voter who has paid attention to all he has said and done since his first inauguration day. His words and actions to get elected were the exact opposite of his actions from the Oval Office since that day, as all his promises to U. S. citizens and voters have been proven lies. This is opinion from a lifetime of observing and, hopefully, preserving what is now in the open, but not reported, much less preserved, by most of the media. Even worse, most of those we have elected to be the people's representatives in our Congress are doing little or nothing about the BHO administrative treason.

What can we do about it? With no positive patriotic majority action from our Congress, maybe the first step is to contact the real news journalists, as well as those who report distorted opinions of news events as often as possible. Rallies, town halls, letters, calls, e-mails, as well as "recall" and "impeachment" petitions are all possible peaceful signals that will help motivate other citizens as well as members of Congress. Making the true danger our country is now facing known to all the reticent and "unknowing," along with the peaceful intent of the majority of patriot citizens and friends, could form a very firm and positive message to the criminals destroying our country! Eventually, even the media lap dogs will have to join in to save face, or face non-entity entirely.

All the events of the past decade or more illuminate how once patriotic, sincere, and honest political parties have absorbed the corruptive influences that have brought the radical philosophies and terrorists into our governmental operations. Fortunately, patriotism is still the function of the majority in most political groups. They need all the help we, the rest of the people, can give to eradicate the Obama disease in the "unknowing" and in others who might think of joining the radical Obama gravy train!

A possible, very public, person in the "unknowing" group, pumping the Obama balloon, is our nation's current Vice President, Joe Biden! Not only has he had both feet in his mouth much of the time in the Obama regime, it is reported that he recently spent over a half million dollars of U. S. tax revenue for a one night stay in a Paris hotel!

It appears the elected are thumbing their noses at taxpayers and making it plain that they don't give a damn about waste, fraud and debt. Biden, reportedly, then went on to London and ran up close to a million dollars for a night or two there. That man continues to excel at public stupidity!

The U. S. has embassies or consulates in almost every major city in the world where Biden, Obama, and all major officials could stay, which are already paid for with tax funds and, most likely, have better security than any hotel, or maybe not in Obama's world if Ben Ghazi is an example. Maybe Biden's intelligence level at math is limited, or his patriotism is of the thought, "that is just pocket change," since Obama's revenue czars keep borrowing trillions from foreign sources, which future generations will never be able to repay.

Why haven't Sandy victims and needy vets benefited from some of the borrowed trillions instead of paying for the Mayor Bloomberg "come to NY" ads? Why hasn't a portion been used to help the unemployed and homeless? The anti U. S. chief spender in our White House prefers supporting those governments, which have many times said they hate the U. S. and will wipe us off the Earth's map! Those are the brilliant minds elected as President and Vice President of the United States in 2008!

The long timers in the "gimme" groups, such as welfare, illegals, lifetime students, incarcerated felons and career unemployed had better figure out that Obama's gravy train has drained the pockets of working taxpayers. Seniors deserving, collecting or near the age of collecting from the Social Security and Medicare programs they paid into will see those funds disappear with the speed of light when the overload of the borrowing and the Obamacare fraud hits everyone under Obama's tyrannical rule.

The self-serving—elected for decades by the hands out, "gimme" robots and those brainwashed by the "my-way-or-no-way" biased and "politically correct" educators who teach the teachers—have shown no conscience, much less allegiance to their country, as they loaded their multi-million dollar bank accounts, through lobbyists and tax revenue scams to waste taxpayer earnings. That was not what the Founders of this nation had in mind when they wrote of the "individual right of freedom and happiness for all."

The time has come for the anti-American philosophy spouted by the first anti-American President, Barack Obama, to stop. I, and others who feel as I do, want him to take his socialist policy of "share the wealth" (you share all you have) and to any of those places with that failed government corruption. True patriots of this country will not stand for the stupidity Obama and the legislative traitors dish out. Those politically correct phonies can get in the exit line along with the B.H.O. group for the next one-way space flight.

It is not the legal, Constitutional, nor moral right of the federal government in our country to determine who can or cannot not enter into a marriage contract. It is each individual U. S. sovereign state's right to make that determination.

It is not in the U. S. federal government's power—legal, Constitutional, or moral—to determine what individual age or illness deserves treatment or which does not. That is the decision of that individual, and/or the individual's doctor, according to the law of the state in which that individual resides.

It is not legal or Constitutional for the U. S. federal government to determine anything an individual citizen must or must not eat or drink or purchase. That is each individual's decision to make within the law of the state where they reside.

It is not Constitutional or in the federal government's power to question or interfere in any way with a state's lawful judicial duties, verdicts, or punishments.

These are just a few of the observations of events or actions I have heard or read about. They could be simplified versions or possibly nowhere near accurate versions. The basic point is that most of the laws enacted in the last three or four decades, voting citizens know little or nothing about. And yet, we are legally bound to abide by them even if the media reported on the "public" version.

chapter 5

NOW—THE END OF WHAT?

In today's world, most of the D. C. legislation being enacted into law by those people we elect to represent us is purposely kept from a vote by the legal residents of our country. That is particularly dangerous as the major proposals could drastically change the daily lives of U.S. citizens. One example is the disastrous Obamacare medical care reform law created by elected and appointed idiots.

In the decades since WWII, the constituents of most of the state and D. C. legislators have been party to less and less information about what our government representatives do "for us" and our country to earn their pay even though communication technology has expanded into outer space.

My memory of "news" in my early teen years is the attack on Pearl Harbor and the wartime events afterwards. The only political names that penetrated my self-centered young brain at that time were FDR and Truman and, of course, the monsters Hitler and Mussolini. The attitude of nearly everyone in that period was pure patriotism that as far as I knew had nothing to do with "political parties." News to me was the war, my brother, words spoken on radio and in film by FDR, Truman, Edward R. Murrow, and my favorite movie stars. The concerns of early age teen females did not relate to anything much past the end of our noses unless some of our male classmates made a particular impression. Probably basic human nature of all ages is more or less the same now as then but progress of technical advantages is so advanced that "learning"—both good and bad—has advanced into much younger human minds. That learning has brought almost subliminal changes in human attitudes. Any advancement in learning has brought good and bad, depending upon the attitude of the mind doing the teaching from the time of birth.

This nation, known as the United States of America since its founding, was created by immigrants for the benefit of other immigrants seeking the basic human individual freedoms provided by God for human happiness, which were not allowed in many other cultures on our planet Earth. Through the more than 235 years since the first pioneers settled on these shores, individuals have established families and prospered through their own talent and effort with the God-given philosophies and policies of the documents this nation's founding ancestors created for we, the people of the United States of America, to enjoy and abide by until the end of time.

This nation was not established for immigrants to replace, change or modify the freedoms offered by this nation, to conform to any other place from which they may have lived.

Unfortunately, throughout our country's history, there have been those who have arrived not approving of the freedoms offered by God and our Founding documents. Some anti-"American freedom" outside influences have slowly infiltrated the education systems, policies, laws, standards, traditions, political parties, and morals of the freedom loving countries on this planet!

Since WWII this nation and others have documented evidence of the disease (with the misnomer "politically correct" attitude) that has created corruption and fraud in all levels of human, social, political, and governmental levels of our daily lives. Outside, or more accurately, radical influences are at the root of demands the basic foundation traditions of our country be eliminated, such as the use of "God" on public buildings and money as well as in the Pledge of Allegiance and the National Anthem! Individual belief in any religion using the name "God," "Allah," "Buddha," or any other name is just one of the many freedoms offered by this the Founders of this nation. If any individual or group does not agree with the founding basics of this country they are welcome to go to a place with other policies and beliefs! God is the creator of this nation! Love it or leave it!

That radical corruption has invaded all three branches of U. S. national operating procedures. Though unthinkable, even the Judicial branch of this nation's framework is no longer pure as the driven snow! One example is the Supreme Court judicial ruling that marriage is not a binding of one each of the two human sexes to perpetuate procreation, but now may include the coupling of two human individuals of the same sex who may or may not perpetuate happiness.

This Supreme Court ruling not only overrules the Constitutional rights of states to determine judgment of marriage decisions in our country but dismisses the natural action of four—and two-legged animal purpose of procreation capability between opposite sexes presumed as the biological, as well as legal, purpose of the marriage contract. A legal civil union contract would serve the purpose of legal happiness between two of the same sex since procreation is impossible. That Judicial judgment is a prime, very high level, example of citizen and state abuse by Federal Justice Department government control corruption.

Another example would be the Federal Judicial ruling against a U. S. state, which mandated by state law a procedure to protect citizens from the illegal act of undocumented people crossing our Federal unsecured national borders. Some of these illegal trespassers come to take advantage of all this nation offers through taxpayer funding, and others to commit additional criminal acts, such as the uncontrolled and ongoing drug running and murder of U. S. citizens in Arizona and other border states and territories.

The Constitutional standards and laws of this nation have never condoned, approved, or permitted any act of treason, such as the "fast and furious" operation sanctioned by any Attorney General and the Justice Department of this nation. Another, more recent treasonous act by the State Department was the ignoring of documented threats and lack of security protection for one of our U. S. ambassadors and other American citizens in U. S. consulates in Egypt and Ben Ghazi, Libya resulting in the murder of the ambassador and other Americans!

Those are just a drop in the ocean of broken laws of our nation allowed to be committed by the politically-correct, criminal, anti-American President and members of the Congress since January 20, 2009.

The elected members of both houses of Congress subscribe to the policies of two long time major "democratic" policy political parties and a few other smaller more recent parties with slightly different basic policies. In the decades since WWII, legal citizens who voted to elect those members of Congress, have had a far more diminished capacity in their right of vote on the multi-mega increase in the proposed legislation which has been enacted by those elected members of our Congress for many, many years.

In that same time frame and, especially in the last couple of decades, legal voting citizens have routinely had their taxes consistently increased to fund our government's operations, and yet, have not obtained the stated objectives for which their representatives were voted into Congress to achieve. They have also seen their earned tax dollars increasingly support the "free" program abusers much more than aid the needy, again without a vote of legal, taxpaying citizens.

The citizens of this country are now the target of a very huge increase in government control of our daily lives for one very important reason. The majority of elected members of our U. S. Congress are no longer doing the job of serving the people who elected them. They are using tax funds paid in to serve their own ambitions, and are now allowing the breaking of U. S. laws and Constitutional documents.

The Founders of our country envisioned and set up a governmental system of three branches: Executive, Judicial, and Legislative. Basically, the purpose of each branch was to check and balance the actions of the others. Simply put, the Executive proposes, the Legislative creates or enacts, the Judicial determines legality—both contemporary and Constitutional. The Executive then signs into law or creates law or action by prescribed limited "Executive Action."

However, the three branches of our government are today not doing their Constitutionally-bound duty for this nation or the legal citizens of this country.

The legislative members of the Congress have allowed thousands of Executive actions without knowing what they are or do, if they are legal, if they benefit or hurt the democratic process of our country, without a vote of the people!

The legislative members of the U. S. Congress have allowed, or made proposals into law, which benefit particular government employees and not the whole legal voting populace.

Our Congressional members have allowed proposals to be added to laws that have nothing to do with the attached law—again, without a vote of the people.

The legislative members of Congress have allowed, or made proposals into law, which benefit only particular governmental employees and not the whole legal voting populace.

It is completely within the power of the Legislative Branch to control any anti-American or criminal actions involving the other two branches of our U. S. government. The members of the U. S. Congress have not done their duty regarding the criminal actions of the Obama administration as of April 1, 2013.

The Judicial branch of the U. S. government consists of appointees of sitting Presidents. The purpose of the Supreme Court Judges, who remain on the bench until they either die or retire, is to uphold laws or determine if particular actions or laws are legal, according to our U. S. democratic process. They do not make laws.

In most administrations, with the appointment by the sitting President, of Supreme Court judges, a balance of political party affiliation is assumed to have been an objective by the voting public, but that effort is not always achieved. The current Supreme Court, with several appointments by the sitting President, is not party affiliation balanced.

The administrative appointees of U. S. government department leaders by elected Presidents are expected to have presidential party affiliation.

I have simplified the above procedures as samples of our country's governmental process, which with research and observation, has shown changes from the founding documents to more political party policy procedures, especially in the Obama administration. This brings to light the changes in the policies of the long time U. S. major political parties.

Patriotism throughout the United States was 100% during WWII, which reached its climax of victory following VJ day! We were a one-for-all and an-all-for-one population without a thought of political party loyalty. It was total happiness as well as a struggle to get back to normal lifestyles after all the deaths, bans, restrictions, shortages, and rationings in our beloved United States.

I have not researched the dates each of the several political parties was established in our country. The two major ones—Democratic and Republican—have always, in theory, focused on keeping our nation operating in the best ways possible for the good of the country.

The only basic differences with other smaller parties has been minor differences in the policies or philosophical beliefs. That said, all U. S. political parties were formed with the same intention: to accomplish actions and benefits for the good of our whole country and all U. S. citizens as well as other freedom-loving people in the process.

It is hard to pinpoint when anti-American influences began undermining political party objectives. It is the same, hard to determine when the purpose in creating labor unions to prevent abuse of child labor, expanded into the expense and promotion of self-serving special interests. The term "lobbyists" came into being, seemingly, for the same purpose.

As I have observed, the policy of the Republican Party is to "go along to get along," or "don't rock the boat." Most of all, they believe "don't spend if you have no money." These are all good philosophies, but can be very restrictive in a progressive and technical world. Simply put, the Republican Party may have become somewhat "careful," "hesitant," "out of touch" or "wimpy."

The Democratic Party's policy seems to have moved in the opposite direction. For some time a path of "spend more to get more" has been the path followed. "Don't worry about the cost." "Let's give some to this one; it might work now." "Add this to that. No one will notice." "There is too much there. Take some of that and put it here."

The shell game of too much or too little with party politics of both major parties has gone on for decades with the resulting policy of "take from the "rich and give to the poor" creed of foreign political parties, not the "you get what you earn" philosophy of the American immigrant entrepreneur!

As descendants of the immigrants who earned, prospered, shared, and passed along to others, we are to blame for not paying attention to the corruption of our once workable government process. We are now suffering with those results.

The elected Congress is riddled with self-serving corruption. The framework of the multi-layered governmental operation is overloaded with unknown and unneeded duplication, fraud, graft, and cost to taxpayers as, over time, administrations have seemingly come to serve some foreign philosophy alien to this country's founding documents and policies. This nation now must take positive peaceful action to reverse the corrosion and corruption or cease to exist altogether! Each citizen must look into the mirror and decide if they want our free nation to survive, or not. Most citizens are true patriots and will do whatever, whenever is necessary to help save our nation from oblivion!

The U. S. government now, in part, has become a dependent or "parent" nation with some of the population believing they were born to be cared for with government funding—the taxes other citizens have worked for and paid to the government. Those citizens or residents are the result of generations of laziness or "you do it!" beliefs. The philosophy of many is if you can't find a job, welfare and unemployment is available.

It will take action in many directions to regain all we have lost, but we have many intelligent and totally patriotic leaders in our nation's varied political affiliations capable of working together. That is the only way we can do what must be done to re-educate and preserve our country with the individual freedoms our Founders created.

Maybe the first step would be to clean the corrosion from our Congress. They need to do that since Constitutionally each branch oversees the others. That is mandated to clear the corruption in our government operating procedures. If they do not do it, they are not patriots of the United States.

Hopefully, every one of us—voting citizens—will also look in the mirror and decide if we are true patriots or not. Each of us must choose either an alien political view, or this nation's original foundation principles laid out by the documents that have been a beacon for others for so many years.

The bottom line for everyone who loves and appreciates all God has given us is to use only plain common sense from this day forward. Hopefully, the media will be able to grow some patriotic spine in order to state the daily facts instead of their usual fiction. If not, they deserve to be the failures they are now. The true journalists are already being heard and heeded.

From what I see and hear daily, most people are unaware, don't care, or are just silently hoping the situation is not as bad as common sense tells them it is! What no one says or wants to believe is that we have elected a President who is trying to completely change the structure of the United States and not for the better! Barack Obama has trashed our nation's Constitutional laws, made new laws, overspent tax funds, and over borrowed on all assets, connived with national enemies, and alienated allies, all without legislative lawful national authorization. In the days of Democratic Presidents FDR, Truman, Kennedy, and probably others, some of the documented and hidden actions of Barack Obama would have been considered acts of a traitor to the country he was elected to serve, protect, defend, and lead!

Not only has the legal voter been lied to by our leaders, but they also have secretly been stripped of individual rights as well as state rights by eliminating national rights with the wrongful use of the legislative as well as the legal systems in our homeland. Not only have some voting rights been usurped or eliminated, but the manipulations have also infringed on our individual privacy to a massive extent. Existing laws are completely changed in intent by the addendums tacked on by self-serving and special interest lobbyists as well as the elected lawmakers in daily voting actions by Congress without the public ever knowing, much less by a vote of we, the people! More than 15,000 pages of new/additional regulations have been signed onto the Obamacare medical care law of 2011 alone.

Access to individual citizens' financial records and assets, in varied degrees, is now available to governmental operations. Individual private and public communication assets are also open in some degree to outside or governmental invasions. This may mean every use we make of the communication air waves, telephone, internet, radio, and television, will be open to governmental intrusions and/or control! Has this been fully disclosed to the public? If not, why not? Has there been any discussion by "governmental operating procedures" to bring any of the above to a vote of we, the people? If not, why not?

The manipulation of each individual citizen's basic Constitutional rights is being manipulated by the intentional perversion of the meaning of all the Constitutional amendment wordings. The "religion" basics have been distorted by non-Christian or anti-religion radicals with the "political correctness" mania.

The right of family, home, and asset protection, or weapon ownership, is being distorted and usurped by self-serving legislators as well as the politically incorrect that emerge from the woodwork whenever there is a criminal shooting of innocents. Proposals against legal gun ownership not only encourage criminals but limits legal individual protection and all law enforcement protective service as well.

Stupidity runs amuck in our citizenry, and in the control supremacy of government with tax funded departments, such as the "Environmental Protection Agency," which protects bugs, weeds, and dead trees ahead of people. That agency encroachment power endorses scientifically disproven scams, (global warming), the financial fiascos of vehicle fuel (corn ethanol), tax fund billions down the drain in solar and wind power bailout disasters and six figure electric cars which might go as much as 150 miles before needing a charge, all on the taxpayers' backs. Fortunately, all the above is true or it could be considered science fiction.

Welcome to "Obamaland" where legal taxpayer tickets now cost nearly $53,000 per man, woman, and child and rising daily. Illegal and amnesty residents have home free admission.

Someone could make a fortune writing a book "Serfdom for Dummies," which should be mandated reading for every U. S. taxpayer. It would be published by the Feds and probably be named a best seller. It should be given to all illegal students and residents.

Just keep believing in those who hand out the free stuff, and don't wake up America. True Patriots will give the best wake up call to everyone.

What is the truth of the situation in our country after almost five years with Obama in the White House? Has the economy become stagnate or rotten? Is there high unemployment with many who have given up job hunting? Are those who are working minimum wage jobs or part time with limited hours and no benefit possibilities? Are job providers fewer? Have some large companies or corporations either moved out of our country or radically cut expenses because of increases in regulations, rules, taxes and fees? Have small businesses made drastic changes in number of employees or gone out of business altogether?

To summarize, Obama has lied to the citizens of our country over and over again and probably throughout his public life. As a candidate for the office of President of the U. S., he first lied by not providing the necessary documentation that he fulfilled all the qualifications for the highest office in our country. The elected representatives of all voting citizens—the U. S. Congress—allowed that first lie by omission, so all members of Congress committed that crime along with the fraudulent President.

This President made many campaign promises before his first inauguration. Those campaign lies have been repeated over and over again by him and others since that day. His initial appointment of cabinet members whose histories included documented law breaking. Later events flaunted major crimes of broken national Constitutional laws of our country that caused many deaths and injuries of our citizens and others actions that I consider nothing less than treason. Again, and again Congress has done nothing.

Ignoring the true facts of the many criminal actions and non-actions and the continued blatant lies by the Obama administration is treasonous behavior by some of our Congress members. The media lost what little integrity of journalistic honesty and truth it had to support the control and corruption of a once major political party in our country. The corrupted media is complicit in those treasonable acts against this country by editing or non-reporting the true and full facts.

I know the brains will laugh at my simplification, but I hope it will bring strong discussion by citizens to develop a foundation to eliminate the evils that have surfaced through the policies and actions of Barack H. Obama. We need to return our country to the vision created by our Founding Fathers.

The bottom line for this nation and possibly the rest of this Earth is that Obama is a not just a bold liar many times over, but he is the icon for criminal corruption in any Constitutional freedom loving society. He was elected President by voting citizens without verified documentation of his qualifications to be President of this nation. Therefore, he is a fraudulent President. The self serving, me first members in our Congress and state governments who allowed that to happen are very much charter members of the "Corruption Party"!

The Barack H. Obama pledge to transform our nation is in allegiance with the roster of basic, contemporary, Constitutional and moral laws he has broken in addition to the blatant crimes of his administration of which he has knowledge of and has obviously condoned.

The actions seem to fall under many headings. Anyone could be aware of most events even with limited news reporting. The actions and non-actions of the legislators speak volumes. But, what do I know? It is just my opinion as I am one worried and frightened citizen.

I believe President Roosevelt and President Truman might ask some legislators what is the legal standing for the "fast and furious" action of Attorney General Eric Holder and the Justice Department? Another question might be: when our sovereign territories in Benghazi, Libya and Egypt were attacked—possible acts of war—why was no reprisal, support or protection provided?

Where are those leaders whose responsibility it is to safeguard U. S. citizens against all those evils, including illegally spying on honest individual citizen's privacy rights through their communications, banking or investments, unless we are under suspicion of breaking laws as the IRS has done? What is being done to provide legal action and charges to stop the spying by the FBI or other government agency on law abiding private citizens, the HHS debacles, and the mandated atrocity written by unknown medical illiterate office staff of elected leaders, most of whom have the same level of medical knowledge?

The repetitive listing the many whys that could be asked is useless. The goal and cure for the Barack Obama problem is a true education for all. Politically-based education in a Constitutional, freedom based society—taught at any and all education levels—is dishonest, immoral, and historically proven failure bound in every place it has been used on planet Earth.

We, the people, the citizens, the voters—whose ancestors came to this country hoping to attain the freedoms for which this nation was created—are responsible for allowing the crimes of our elected leaders through the decades, especially those committed during the Barack Obama years, are taking from all future generations the freedoms bestowed by God on humanity during the evolution of this land known as America.

AFTERWORD

History is always being made. Unfortunately, not all history has been documented and preserved. The last decade or more has brought to light some unfortunate facts regarding our comparatively young nation in the life of human history. Fortunately, both good and bad facts in history are available to be learned, as well as enriched throughout time.

Since the founding of our country, the abolishment of most slavery on planet Earth ended. Outer space exploration and travel became possible in the mid-20th Century along with scientific, mechanical, and technical achievements—dreams of a few just a few short years before.

In the first decade of the 21st Century the erasure of color lines in the U. S. was achieved with the election of Barack Obama as President. Unfortunately, shortly thereafter the citizens and residents of our nation were confronted with the burst of the economic boom bubble in the late '90s.

The world has since experienced dire consequences. Our nation has come within sight of oblivion through the disregard of our Founding principles, laws, and documents by our elected leaders. For several decades our country has not been governed by the founding basics for a free humanity. King George III would be applauding the tyrannical progression allowed and promoted by the leaders of our nation in recent years.

Treason has been ignored in word and deed by those entrusted with the protection of all freedoms bequeathed to the immigrants of the world who have become citizens of the United States and dared to dream the dream.

Truth and honesty in politics throughout the world, as well as our beloved nation, has been replaced by the embedded manipulation of self-ambition and greed through the eons of human development. That infection has been spread through the illiterate and lazy for centuries. The historical repetition of government in control of the people, instead of the people controlling government, is the operating procedure in our country now.

The reality of the world situation, including our homeland, has not been absorbed by many with focus on daily life. An escape into the reality TV exploits, idiotic activities and quotes from Hollywood, or other wannabe celebrities, blinds much of what many do not understand or would rather not know.

For many decades the media news concentration, mainly through the alphabet networks, has been the 24/7 coverage of sitcom-type murders, drive-by crimes, or the scandals of selected celebrities, politicians, or sports names and teams.

Coverage of major events by the alphabet networks routinely consists of opinions in place of true facts in news presented to the public. That may mean political bias of favored politicians' self-promoting legislation proposals, in place of true journalism. The networks and radio which have journalistic pride are tuned out by the uncaring idiots in favor of flamboyant statements by questionable IQ politicians, and other celebrity mouths.

I believe, and hope, that true U. S. Patriots of Freedom will come together peacefully to end the governmental tyranny. They will use the principles and freedoms embraced by our Founders to once again return our nation to its rightful place as the shining beacon of leadership that no other government has ever attained.

What does it mean when the individuals we elect to be our leaders care more for the politics than the patriotic? The enormous scale of the greed, deception, and just plain stupidity in our government, which has come to light, is mind boggling!

Hindsight opens a lot of eyes as well as the wounds of the blame game. The resulting aftermath is incomprehensible to most honest people. I am just one of the many who share the same observations, conclusions, and fear of worse things as a result of greed and evil. God bless our nation's freedom for all individual family life and help us preserve the United States for all freedom loving humanity.

In God we trust!